Sessy's Journey

By
Shirley Sanders

2014
Bookspurdee Publisher

Published in the United States
by
Bookspurdee Publisher

P.O. Box 531538
Henderson, Nevada 89053

Manufactured in the Unites States of America

For information on special discounts and bulk purchases, contact Bookspurdee at (855) 792-9285

The Library of Congress has catalogued this paperback edition.

Sanders, Shirley
Sessy's Journey will spark the emotional side of you allowing you to go from crying to laughter and back again.

1. Black history. 2. Biography. 3. Christian. 4. Ethnic-history

ISBN: 978-0-9895931-0-6

Dedication

In Memory of my parents:
James and Frances (Walker) Pittman.

To my children:
Felecia Baptiste and Robyn Sanders.

To my siblings:
Leroy Pittman, Lucille Roberts,
Christene Fortenberry, Wade Zebedee Pitman

and,
all the mothers that had to bury their children.
May God's blessings forever shine on you.

Acknowledgments

I thank Almighty God who through my ancestors gave me the will and the way to live my life this way.

I especially give honor and respect to my mother and father who did not have a formal education, but were smart and faithful individuals who expressed love and taught me the basis of life.

To my siblings Leroy, Lucille, Christine, and Zebedee for allowing me to think that I was the boss of the family and holding it together like Mama had asked of me. Forgive me if I took it too far sometimes.

My niece Eunice who traveled to my home from afar to assist me in getting this book started. She is an awesome web designer who designed my website. Thanks Eunice for helping me to get over the fear of that dreaded computer.

To my daughters Felecia and Robyn thanks for pushing me when I felt like giving up and filling in the spaces that I had forgotten.

Thank you Zebedee and Charlemaine for all the nutritious meals that you shared with me that allowed me to eat well and keep on working on this project.

Thanks to my editor Denice Whitmore who guided me through this project and made me feel I did it myself. Your assistance made a big difference in getting to the finish line.

Thank you Jaqui Jefferson, my honest critic for keeping it real.

Without the assistance of Carrie Laurant who made sure that all the T's were crossed and all the I's got dots and helped me calm down my Southern accent this project could not have been completed.

To my Tai Chi and church friend, Bernice, for her support and catching me before drowning in my trials and tribulations, believe me there were many. You are always there.

Special thanks to my Tai Chi Master Bilal Amin for his instructions that kept my body soul and mind in perfect balance. And the self-defense classes that gave me a sense of security and peace.

Many thanks Ron and Cynthia Dellums for your friendship and providing me with a quiet place to write, and all your superb hospitality which made my life better.

Priscilla, dear Priscilla, your input will never be forgotten. You have lifted me up so many times, I stopped counting. All I can say is thank you.

Al and Ann, the both of you were right there

for me doing things that I had no idea how to do and you did it well. I am so glad that you are my cousins.

Ella, my friend in time of need. When I lost my desire for gardening you came and revived it so that I could continue my project thanks.

Georgia my prayer partner thanks for your continued prayers.

Shedeem, your computer classes were the best. I am proud to have a grandson like you.

Thanks to Alphonso King, my photographer, who worked wonders on the old photographs that I gave him.

All of you that I did not name, you know who you are. Thank you, thank you and be blessed.

Introduction

My aspiration for writing this book began after my 80th birthday celebration. This big event gave some insight to the life I had lived and in such a matter of fact way. I realized that I had something to say.

Being born to parents with little education but rich in good morals gave me the roots that I needed to make this journey. They allowed me to spread my wings at age fifteen. I practiced their teaching as I went on my way.

I soon learned about the tough times that made me strong and the reward of being honest, compassionate and truthful.

I write for those who have had to bury their child. And those who have fallen down and refuse to get up. A man is not a failure until he blames his failure on someone else.

Traveling this journey more than eight decades gave me some insight about life's up's and down's.

It is my pleasure to share my story, not for pity but to acknowledge the fact that faith in God can create a humane and brave individual.

When you read this book you will understand everything. So read the book and be blessed.

Table of Contents

Table of Contents
(Cont.)

Sessy's Journey

Chapter 1
Making a Way

S mack! I felt my lip swelling before I hit the floor, butt first. Alvin stood over me with his fist clenched as he waited for me to get up. I stayed down, knowing that if I did get up, he would hit me again. He waited a moment before stepping over me. When he did, he brushed his foot across my leg with a slight push that meant he was the victor. I had endured this abuse for over ten years. I felt like such a weak fool accepting this awful treatment.

It was Alvin's day off and I wondered what today's excuse would be for him to get out of the house for the entire day.

Alvin said, "Sessy, my brother is coming to pick me up. He wants me to go to San Francisco to help him take care of some kind of business." He fidgeted with his gold tie clip, centering it on his neck tie. He was dressed in a blue plaid suit, white shirt with gold cuff links and shiny black shoes. Oh yes, he was a sharp dresser seven days a week. He was a tailor for a large department store and everything had to fit to a T. He said, "I'm not sure when I'll be back". I looked at him with that 'I don't believe you look' but said nothing. Oh well, he had his secrets and I had mine.

1

This was the summer of 1976 and my marriage of 23 years was a disaster. My husband Alvin acted as though it didn't matter. He felt like he had complete control. We were the parents of six children. Our sons had joined the military and the girls were teenagers, still living at home.

I had an hour before opening the beauty shop attached to the back of the house. I checked my schedule and gathered the tools and supplies I needed for my first customer. I made one last check around the shop to make sure everything was tidy. This shop was the source of my income and my escape from reality.

My mind wandered as I worked. I suffered from empty nest syndrome. I really missed the boys. It had been well over a year since I'd seen them.

My Mama's words echoed in my head. 'Sessy, where there's a will, there's a way.'

I chuckled to myself. Girl, don't be silly.

My first patron of the day interrupted my thoughts. "Good morning Miss Brown. You look nice today."

"Oh girl, stop lying. Just wait 'til I take this hat off." We both had a good laugh and the day went on as usual.

After work, I thought about the boys again and my secret plan. I wrote to them some time ago and expressed my feelings. I wished so much to go and visit. They had been my world for so long. As we exchanged letters, I longed to see where they lived, meet their families and experience the things they wrote about. So I hatched a plan to go for a visit. Why couldn't I have this one thing, just for me?

Jerry, our oldest, and Tony, our youngest, were very happy about my plan. They said, "Mother wait until we find out if you are eligible to fly military rates. It will cost you less".

Just work on getting your passport for now."

Getting my passport was a problem. My name was different on my birth certificate. I was told my name is Sessy, but my name was spelled Susie Mae. They chose to put both names on the passport so at least one of them would match my driver's license. The day I received my passport, I screamed and shouted. Now I could visualize my trip to South Korea to see my boys.

I set the date of my trip in July to coincide with the girl's schedule. They were dependable teenagers, thirteen, fifteen and seventeen. They could live through one month on their own. Plus they needed to experience life without me.

I told a few of my close friends of my secret plan. They commended me for being so brave. They formed a group to help me make this grand trip. I received luggage, toiletries, money, clothing and shoes.

Everything was set and ready to go in two weeks. Time was closing in on me. I would have to break it to Alvin. I knew he would gripe and call it a foolish idea.

After dinner that night, he looked to be in a fairly good mood. I blurted it out. If he decided to hit me, I would just go to Korea with a black eye. Nothing he could do would stop me now.

"Hey Alvin, guess what? I got a chance to go see Jerry and Tony in Korea."

"What? I know you must be kidding." He dropped his fork and stared at me across the table. "Are you crazy? Where is the money coming from?"

"They went to whoever is in charge and got me military rates. It will not cost that much." I returned his stare, showing a confidence I didn't feel.

"I cannot take off work to see about these kids" he said.

"You won't have to. They know how to cook and take care of the house. I assigned them two days each and Saturday is a go for yourself day."

I endured Alvin's catty remarks for a few days. He could not give me a good reason to stay home. This would be my first taste of freedom. I was determined to enjoy my vacation.

I left the confines of my home in Berkeley, California and headed out for the long flight to South Korea. My feelings were mixed; sad to leave the girls, ecstatic about leaving Al, and excited to finally see my sons, Tony and Jerry.

I boarded the plane in San Francisco, took my seat and rested my head into the fluffy pillow the stewardess gave me. I wasn't really looking forward to the long flight. I would make a short stopover in Hawaii, and then through customs in Japan and finally on to my final destination, Seoul, Korea.

After 18 hours of shifting and twisting in my seat, the plane began its descent. My eyes enveloped the beauty of Seoul's massive island coast. It was amazing--different from the Hawaiian coast, where the water seemed to take over and command respect, with roaring waves and different hues of blue. Seoul's abundance of land surrounded by smaller bodies of water, peacefully exposed beautiful mixtures of blue stillness. Hawaii's land was engulfed with tall palm trees. But Korea's hillsides and mountains were smooth, as though they had been shaved by a huge lawn mower and painted with a big brush of green. Trees were minimal, but there were interesting formations amongst the greenery, which I would later find out, were several strategically placed burial tombs.

The plane landed and I fidgeted in anticipation of seeing my sons for the first time after a long year and meeting Tony's new wife, Ling-Su. I took the short walk through the tunnel connected to the plane which lead to the terminal, I saw Tony with his wife, Ling-Su, Jerry and his wife Sung-Ja and Nicole, my three-year-old granddaughter.

My arms flew from one body to the next, squeezing with every ounce of my love. I cried tears of happiness and our voices squealed with joy.

Tony introduced me to his wife, Ling-Su, a beautiful Korean girl. She was tiny and neatly dressed, her skin flawless and she had a certain glow about her. She appeared to be shy and I knew I would love her as my own daughter.

I had met Sung-Ja in the states. She and Jerry got married in our home. A year later she gave birth to Nicole. Sung-Ja spoke fluent English, but Ling-Su spoke very little.

On the way to Jerry and Sung-Ja's house, they gave me a mini tour of the country-side, and educated me on some of their culture. I saw the bustling city both modern and ancient with its new buildings and ancient temples. We drove past a school. The field looked like it was covered in a giant blue blanket.

"What is that on the field over there?" I asked.

"Those are the students in their physical fitness class," Sung-Ja told me.

What an amazing sight to behold. The children wore their blue school uniforms and moved together creating the illusion of fabric floating in the breeze.

Once in the house, the aromatic fragrance of Korean cooking caught my attention. The maid scurried about to set the food up for the family. Traditionally, the Korean people eat while seated on the floor at a small round table with legs about eighteen inches from the floor. I sat on the floor, looked at the food and thought how different it was from American food. It was so colorful and some of the dishes were questionably curious. Ling-Su had a small plate which was almost covered with soy sauce. She spoke to the maid in Korean and then received a raw egg on top of the sauce. Ling-Su mixed the concoction with her chop sticks and dipped rice into the mixture.

I looked around at everyone eating with his or her chopsticks. "Do you think I could have a fork?" I asked.

"Come on Mom, give it a try. It's not that hard. Like this." Tony proceeded to show me how to hold the chopsticks properly. Everyone gave me advice on the best way. So I gave it a try and dug in for my first bite.

Rice fluttered across the table. I fought with a slice of beef, which lost contact with the chopsticks hitting the ceiling. Everyone broke into hysterics and Jerry yelled, "Give her a spoon! Give her a spoon!"

For the next three weeks, they took me on daily outings. We went from Seoul to Pusan and even the beautiful island of Cheju, known as The Hawaii of the Orient. We went everywhere. Local tour guides led some of the sights we visited.

Cheju was a great island, so different from anything I've ever seen. The volcanoes erupted many years before, leaving porous rocks all over the island. In order to farm the land, the rocks had to be piled into rows, like fences. Some were in big piles and some were used to build houses. In other areas, they were just left where they were because there were too many to move.

The women did all the work, which might explain

the reason why the men were smaller than the women. I watched the women working with hot tar on the highways and it made me a little sad. I got a kick out of watching the Amazon-looking women dive off the cliffs for pearls, abalone, sea grass and beautiful shells.

The men didn't work at all. I felt this was very odd. The men stayed home. Most of them played GO, a checker-like board game.

My favorite tour was the visit to the Chichewa Monks Temple in the foothills of Mt. Hwant-Akson. We climbed up a steep mountain to get there.

Sung-Ja explained the history behind this famous Temple. It was the temple of One Thou-sand Buddha.

When we arrived, a bald female monk greeted us holding a tin pail of water, and a very dirty tin dipper to serve the visitors. I flinched, wondering just how many lips had touched that dipper before us. Sung-Ja and Jerry took a sip and gave it back to the Monk. Oh Lord, it's my turn. Oh well... when in Rome. One sip will not kill me.

When we entered the room that held the One Thousand Buddha, Sung-Ja told me they were made of pure jade. I was expecting to see all green, but they were pure white and evenly spaced. It was very impressive.

Tony said, "I wish I had just one of those. I would never have to work again."

I enjoyed the trip up the mountain. Going down the mountain was much harder. I slid down the mountain a few times but was still in one piece when I reached the bottom.

I was unfamiliar with the Korean currency and its exchange rate. I didn't know how to change American dollars to Korean Won. I gave Sung-Ja four hundred U.S. dollars and she went into her bedroom. She came out with a large bundle of Won. She rolled it into a newspaper on the floor. The wad was too large to fit in her purse, so he put it into a large shopping bag.

Our next trip was to the city of Seoul. We went shopping downtown. Jerry and Tony convinced me that Korea was an underdeveloped country with lots of bargains. The clothes were well made and I got more for my money. My daughters had given me cut out pictures of what they wanted from a Sears Catalog and other magazines. We searched for a while for the things on the list. To my surprise, there was nothing in the store that was remotely similar to what the girls wanted. We decided to get the socks, sweaters and blouses out of the way first. We did the best we could.

The Koreans bodies are shaped much different than Americans and they are much smaller. There were no way any of the pants we found would fit over Pamela's or Jeanine's butt and hips.

Sung-Ja found a shop that would make the girls pants and jackets in time for me to take them home. School would start five days after I arrived home.

Sung-Ja and Ling-Su planned my departure party. They asked me to cook Jerry and Tony's favorite foods--banana pudding for Jerry, and Louisiana seafood gumbo for Tony. Jerry, a concert pianist, and some of his band members, would play for my party. Only a few of the neighbors were invited.

The party was held on the balcony, off the second floor of their home. Many of the uninvited neighbors brought chairs and lined them near the street that faced the house. Sung-Ja said, "It's probably the first time they have witnessed an American Party."

Jerry's Korean officer friend came to the party. He told everyone he could speak English very well. When Jerry introduced us, the officer pasted a big grin across his face, took a bow and said, "Good morning, Sir". "Nice to meet you, Sir."

I returned his greetings. "Thank you. Thank you." I would not dare rain on his parade by informing him that it was 8:00 pm, and I am not a man.

We dined and danced until 11:00 pm.

At midnight, a loud siren went off. To avoid arrest, everyone had to be off the streets immediately. It was as if the city suddenly died. At exactly five o'clock the next morning, it would come to life just as quickly as it died the night before.

I thanked my two daughters-in-law for giving me a wonderful party, assuring them that the memories would be locked in my 'good memory bank' forever.

I really hated leaving Nicole. She was my first grandchild. I was there the first day of her life. She slept with me the first three weeks of her life because Sung-Ja said she didn't know what to do with her,

"She's too small."

Nicole weighed nine pounds!

She was two years old when Jerry and Sung-Ja moved to Korea. During that year, Nicole lost her English words and spoke only Korean.

I was asked to watch Nicole for a few hours and I replied, "Oh yes, I would love to watch her."

It went well for a little while until Nicole asked me for something in Korean.

"What?" I asked.

More Korean words came out of Nicole's mouth.

9

I panicked. Oh Lord, I don't know if this child is asking to eat or go to the bathroom!

I took her to the bathroom. "No!"

I then took her hand and went to the refrigerator to get her a bowl of rice. "No!"

Nicole started crying and I wanted to cry too. A little later Jerry and Sung-Ja returned. Nicole ran and hugged both of them. I never found out what she wanted; she was probably asking, "Where are mommy and daddy?"

Somehow, word got around about the banana pudding that I made for the party. Sung-Ja's beautician wanted to taste some, if she had any leftover. There was none left so Sung-Ja asked me to make more. She then invited her beautician and staff to lunch. They came early and the pudding was still hot.

"It's supposed to be cold."

The women loved it hot and ate too much. It was their first time eating banana pudding and a few hours later, most of them had a bad case of diarrhea.

Making a Way

But thanks be to God, which giveth us the victory
through our Lord Jesus Christ

1 Corinthians 15:57

Chapter 2
Losing Waldo

My visit was coming to an end. Oh how I dreaded the long flight home. On the trip here, going through customs in Japan, I had a bad experience with one of the Customs agents at the airport. This was a very scary moment for me. He opened my luggage, gave me a dirty look and shouted in Japanese. He then picked up my luggage and threw it down as if he wanted to damage it. I hoped someone else would process me on the way home.

From there, I would go back to Hawaii then on to San Francisco.

At the airport, the hugs and kisses were plentiful and saying goodbye was very hard. As I boarded the plane, I took one look back for a final wave and I realized tears were running down my cheeks.

I composed myself and found my way to my seat next to a young black man. "Hello" I said.

"Hello, how are you?" It was just a cordial exchange of words. He quickly conveyed that sleep was on his mind. That was fine with me because I had some thinking to do.

I thanked God for protecting me on this fantastic trip. I could never have imagined myself, this little, plump, five feet, one and a half inch black woman from the fields of Mississippi, born during the Great Depression, being on a

13

trip like this in another country. Yes, there is a God!

I was very tired and had no problem going to sleep soon after takeoff.

We landed in Tokyo some time later. My trip through customs this time was easier. The customs inspector was kind and efficient. Soon, I reboarded the plane and settled in for the long flight to Hawaii.

After several hours in flight, a voice came over the speakers. "This is your pilot speaking. Due to difficulty with the aircraft we must return to Tokyo."

The trip back to Tokyo was like being in hell. Fear engulfed me. My thoughts flew to my three daughters. Is this plane going to fall? I picked the nail polish off three of my nails. What will happen to my kids? Oh yes, Al will be there with them. I began to accept the fact that I could die on this plane.

My mind wandered back to Waldo. I felt the same queasiness in my stomach that I did the night he was killed.

Waldo was our sixteen year old son. I remembered some of the funny things he would do. Like the night before our fifteen state tour in our station wagon.

The girls and I were sitting in the den watching the Tom Jones Show on the television. Waldo entered the room and began popping his fingers to the beat. He rushed to the bathroom to comb his afro. He came back, and pulling me from my chair, he wiggled his legs like Tom Jones.

Without missing a beat he asked if he could go say goodbye to his friend Mike since we were leaving in the morning.

"It's okay with me but you better check with your father first."

14

"Where is he?"

"He is in the station wagon hanging the new curtains I just made. He may need your help."

But Al didn't need his help and told him he could go, "But make it short. We will be getting up early."

This was going to be a great vacation. I started packing the old blue metal footlocker that sat in the den a month before our departure just to be sure we didn't forget anything. Packing for six kids and two adults for a two week adventure was not easy.

Al informed us we would be leaving at seven o'clock sharp the next morning. Everyone was excited about the trip.

Our first stop would be Mississippi, our native home. Then on to Chicago, Illinois to visit Al's sister. We would come home by the northern route.

I looked at the clock at 8:59 pm. The packing was done and the girls and I were finished watching Tom Jones so we went to get ready for bed. I heard voices upstairs. Waldo must have come home. He is talking to Tony upstairs.

Jerry, our oldest son, had a night job at Kellogg's. He would be home in the morning before we got on the road.

Everyone was settled. Al and I were in bed watching the late news around 11:30 when the phone rang. Al answered it. I listened to his end of the conversation.

"He left here about 8:30... Yeah... Yeah... Where? I will be right down."

I sprang from bed, "What is it? Did something happen to Jerry at work?"

Al hung up the phone. His face fell and he looked disturbed. "That was the coroner's office calling, apparently Waldo and Mike were involved in some kind

15

of holdup...and Waldo was shot."

Uncontrollable screams leaped from my mouth. I felt restless like I had to be somewhere--anywhere but there. I paced the room feeling lost. No! Not Waldo! He is upstairs. I heard him talking to Tony.

Hearing my screams, Tony ran downstairs to our bedroom.

"Wasn't your brother upstairs with you?" Al asked him. Tony looked at us in confusion. "Waldo's not upstairs. He went to see Mike, remember?"

I got up. "Let me get my purse. I'll go with you."

"No. I'll take care of this. I will call you as soon as I know something." Tony tried to go with him as well but he refused him.

I was still holding on to the word "shot." People do live after being shot. I could not sit still and wait. I felt an urgent need to be busy, very busy. I started the dishwasher, put clothes in the washing machine and started the dryer, even though there were no clothes in it.

I pulled out the vacuum cleaner. That is when I heard Al pull into the driveway. Tony rushed outside to meet Al. They hugged and they were crying. I did not want to face them when they entered the house. I knew what that crying meant and fled the room so I wouldn't have to face them.

Deep down inside, I knew Waldo was dead. The call would have come from the hospital, not the coroner's office.

I could not sit still. I paced and cried for several hours. I called my sister, Crystal. It felt strange to say the words out loud. "Waldo is dead. He was shot," I sobbed into the phone.

She came right over and tried to calm me down.

16

Nothing worked.

Al decided to call the family doctor, who came and gave me medication. The next morning I looked like I had the measles and the mumps--my face swollen with grief and loss.

The days that followed were unreal--making funeral arrangements, talking to the press, answering questions to friends and well-wishers. I tried to make some sense of Waldo's death. I was baffled. The more I tried to explain it to the kids, the more my confusion and anger grew.

I went to the funeral home to view his body to give approval for the public viewing. I will never forget how cold and clammy his skin felt. How they had combed his hair. He always wore an afro hair style. The owner informed me that he had never combed an afro before, so he combed it straight back and it looked like a tree. I told him I would comb his hair and he should watch me so he would know for himself.

I combed Waldo's hair and spoke to him while fluffing it out. "Waldo, I am so sorry. I am going to miss you Waldo. I will always miss you. I will not let them get away with this. I will fight for you. I will fight! I cannot say goodbye. I love you."

I fought back the bubbles that formed in my throat. I did not want to leave him there in that cold place.

"Please Lord, accept my son into your kingdom."

We held the service at our church, which filled to capacity. The trip to the cemetery was long and hot. I did not accept for myself that Waldo was gone until they lowered his casket and threw dirt on it. I lost my nerve and could not look anymore.

Oh, God. I will never see my child again...This is it.

Never is such a long time.

The trip home was so lonely. I felt like I was the only one in that big car. The traffic outside moved in slow motion. We were somewhere on the highway, on our way home but I did not recognize our surroundings.

We arrived home to a house filled with people.

Oh God, I don't want people! I want to be alone!

This was my time to think about Waldo. The things we did together, the pranks he used to play on me. He had a big smile that softened my heart every day. He helped me in the kitchen when I needed it. He made a mean sweet potato pie. We had a great understanding. I would miss him. I would visit his grave daily if I could fit it into my schedule.

Our house changed. There was a certain uneasiness in our home. Each of the children displayed grief in their own way. Jerry didn't talk much. He just played the piano, in his own little world. Tony was filled with anger and bitterness. It was so contrary to his usual happy-go-lucky personality. He had lost his best friend. Waldo and Tony slept in the same bed for most of their lives.

Pamela, who was eleven at the time, cried a lot and clung to me at times. If someone wasn't in her sight she would become fearful and need reassurance that they were in a safe place and doing fine. Jeanine was nine. She worked out her grief by cleaning the house over and over again. Ellen was seven. She did not know what to do either. She sucked her thumb and spent a lot of time with an elderly couple that lived two doors away.

Al seemed to be the only one going about his life as usual. He went to work daily and to church nightly. I felt he was suffering inside but did not know how to express himself. A man crying is a sign of weakness.

Al professed to being a Christian in the Baptist Church most of his life. He rarely missed an activity at church. He once told me, "Waldo's death was God's will and I don't question God. Blessed be the name of the Lord."

I grew up in the Baptist Church and was active most of my life. My activities consisted of helping the kids in school and being a room mother. I did Boy Scouts, Girl Scouts, and Cub Scout Den Mother and kept up with all of their sports.

I did not share Al's views. I was hurt and very, very angry. I blamed myself for not having enough money or education to fight the police department. Waldo's friend, Mike, had been in jail before. He knew the ropes. When the police shouted "halt," Waldo kept running. He was shot in the back approaching a tall brick wall.

They had already captured Mike. He could have identified Waldo. They didn't have to chase him down. The police labeled his death a 'Justifiable Homicide'. I called it murder.

The summer was long and dreary. With so many changes, I hated to go back to work in the beauty shop. I had taught Waldo how to cut hair, shampoo and do other services in the shop. I would close the shop at noon every Saturday. At 12:30, Waldo would turn it into his barbershop. His customers consisted of his schoolmates and their fathers.

It was a way for Waldo to make money for himself. I encouraged him to open a bank account and save money for college. He was so proud to have his own bank account.

It was time for me to re-open the beauty shop and take care of my customers. The weeks I was closed, I went fishing every day. I wanted to be alone. Going back to

19

work without Waldo was hard for me. I wondered what else I could do with only a few college credits.

I looked in the newspaper hoping to find a job. Any job. I called a few friends asking them to help me in my job search. The daily fishing trips I took were getting boring. Too many uninvited friends were trying to console me. They crowded out my space on the river. I really just wanted to be alone.

So it was decision time. Either go back to work in the shop, or become the neurotic person I was turning into. Going back to school was also an option.

A few weeks later, I enrolled in a nearby Community College and carried fifteen units. My goal was to get an Associate's Degree. None of my previous credits were accepted.

Al was infuriated when I told him. "When are you going to have time to run the beauty shop and take care of the kids? I had better not come home one time to no dinner. Why didn't you tell me first, before you enrolled?"

"Because I knew you would react just like you're doing now. Anyway I've already enrolled."

The days that followed were hectic for me. I had to plan a school schedule, a clientele schedule, the children's schedule and a house keeping schedule.

I was shaken from my thoughts when the pilot made an announcement. "May I have your attention please? We will be landing in Tokyo in twenty minutes. Do not be alarmed by the fire trucks near the runway. It's an extra precaution. The foam on the landing strip will ensure a less bumpy landing.

There was a big jolt. Some of the passengers yelled in

relief and some clapped their hands with sheer joy.

"Ladies and Gentlemen, please remain seated until further notice."

The passenger sitting next to me said, "Oh, hell no! I want to get off of this thing now! God, I need a drink."

"Oh take it easy. God got us down in one piece, didn't he?"

I silently prayed. Thank you for giving me another chance to see my daughters and the possibility of watching them become adults.

After about thirty minutes of waiting, we were told that four tires had blown out during takeoff causing the warning signal to remain on. "Those of you who wish to get off the plane and have snacks or drinks may do so now."

I remained on the plane. After a few more hours, the pilot finally announced, "Thank you for your patience. We will be departing soon...Destination, Hawaii."

We reached Hawaii, where we were told there was something else wrong with the plane. We were asked to deplane and board another plane for our final destination, San Francisco.

I was glad to be home. There really is no place like home. The girls had done a good job of taking care of the house. Even Al pitched in by feeding the dog every day.

Pamela asked me, "How in the world did you do all this work by yourself?"

"It's tough. Real tough" I told her. "Now you know I will be expecting a lot more help from all of you. I left three little girls and came back to find three young ladies."

The girls hated all the clothes I purchased in Korea. Even I had to admit they would look a lot different from all the other kids.

21

School started and the beauty shop opened with a high volume of clients. It did not feel the same. This is when I appreciate the value of my imagination. I can always relive my happy-go-lucky childhood and try to forget the bad times.

I will never forget Waldo.

Losing Waldo

My heart is sore pained within me:
and the terrors of death are fallen upon me.

Psalms 55:4

Chapter 3
Early Childhood Memories

I think about my childhood sometimes. Of all my 82 years, it seems to be the safest, happiest time for me. Mama was born in 1901. She was part Choctaw Indian and part Black. Her long, dark silky hair fell gracefully to the waist of her tall thin frame, all shinny and black. She was soft-spoken, but was no cream puff. Mama was my go to person. I could ask her questions about anything, except sex. "Girl, that's grownup talk, not kids," she would say.

Mama had a way of making me feel special. She always believed in me and encouraged me to reach for higher heights. Mama showed us affection by softly stroking our cheek with the back of her hand. I don't recall her ever hugging or kissing me and yet I knew she loved me.

Daddy was born in 1890 and grew up in a large family with twenty siblings, all from the same mother.

"How in the world did she cook for all those Kids?" we asked him.

"She didn't. She would cook for the smaller ones and the older ones had to cook for themselves," he said.

Daddy was a World War I veteran. Six months into his army duty, he got sick with the flu. In those days influenza was life threatening. He was discharged after he recovered.

Before I was born, in the late twenties, Daddy moved

his growing family from place to place, living in shanty shacks while sharecropping. During the Great Depression, most everyone suffered hardship and deprivation. The whole world was in an uproar. I was born in the spring of 1931 in the state of Mississippi, off Highway 35, halfway between New Orleans, Louisiana and Jackson, Mississippi.

The last landowner that Daddy sharecropped for gave him a new lease on life. This God fearing man informed Daddy of the New Deal created by President Roosevelt. Daddy signed up for the Veterans Benefit called 'The First New Deal.' He received forty dollars.

Both Mama and Daddy were from Louisiana and they were hard-working farmers. They migrated just 12 miles across the state line to Cheraw, Mississippi. Daddy took his forty dollars and bought forty acres of land and moved his family onto land he called 'his own.' The land was full of gullies and rocks. Nevertheless, it was his land to do what he wanted to do. He made good use of the land.

Daddy cleared the land and fenced it in and was ready to move. Everyone in the neighborhood helped build a one-room house. My oldest brother, George also helped build the house. It took less than a week, and what a week it was. The neighbors brought food every day, hearty meals like collard greens, ham hocks, pork chops and cornbread.

Daddy filled the land with fruit trees like cherry, pecan, pear, walnut, apples, plums, peaches and mulberry bushes. Huckleberries and blackberries grew wild in the woods. We had Indian peach trees. This odd peach is blood red on the inside and has grayish fuzz on the outside. It was not sweet and the outside fuzz was a little icky, but Mama made jellies and jams out of it, which made it edible.

26

A year later, Daddy bought five undeveloped acres in front of the house for five dollars. He used the land to grow sugar cane. Another year past and Daddy built a second one-room, larger home--the gravel road paved two years after that.

Eight years past and Daddy built a third house with three bedrooms, living room, dining room and a kitchen. The third home is the one I can remember. The house sat on the side of a hill. Nine steps led to the door of the house. People often asked us if we could stand up in the house. We could stand up under the house, the hill was that steep. With a little ingenuity and a few planks of wood to enclose the bottom area, we could have been the only family that had a two level house. I suppose Daddy could not fathom such a thing. No one in the whole county had two floors.

The front door opened into the living room, which doubled as Mama and Daddy's bedroom. A wood burning potbelly heater sat on the right side of the room, while four wooden chairs were on the left. A standard-size bed sat neatly made with a blue chenille bed cover. On the opposite wall stood a chifferobe that held Mama and Daddy's clothes and important papers. Next to that was a wooden box that held baby clothes.

Curtains hung over the kitchen door. A wood burning stove sat to the right, front of a long picnic style table with a bench on each side. The icebox sat in the corner, next to the "safe," which was a freestanding cabinet that held the dairy products and dishes. The bottom portion held some food and cooking utensils. Daddy had customized the back wall to store all the quart-sized jars of food the family canned for the winter.

I slept in the back room next to the kitchen, between

my sisters, Maxine and Crystal. My brothers, Calvin, Lee and Larry slept in the room next to ours.

Outside, near the kitchen, was a smokehouse used to smoke ham, bacon and homemade sausage. A huge wooden box sat next to the window that held slabs of pork belly, saturated in layers of salt used as a curing agent to keep the salt pork from spoiling. An oak smoke stack smoldered in the middle of a dirt floor. Racks hung above with homemade sausage and hams, smoked to perfection.

A few feet to the right of the shack sat a huge pile of dirt in the shape of an igloo, where the sweet potatoes were stored. Daddy and my brothers poured the sweet potatoes into the pine straw lined hole and piled them up four or five feet high. We packed pine straw firmly over the stack, then shoveled dirt over the straw in a thick layer. This dirt kept the damaging element out.

To the left was the chicken shed, the nighttime roosting place for the chickens and the egg laying receptacles. Daddy placed four ladders for the chickens to climb up to racks that went across the back of the room. Just outside of this shack is where Mama's huge fenced-in garden lay.

Mama grew a large vegetable garden that added to all the fruit from the trees throughout the farm. In the woods grew wild berries, mahaws, muscadines, and persimmons, which Mama used to make jams and jellies. She also made medicines from wild herbs the same way her mother used to make. She took pride in this garden, growing a wide variety of food. The tomatoes and onions were her specialty.

She would enter them in the county and 4-H Club fairs. She never won a ribbon. She always felt cheated when they gave out the ribbons. She later realized that she was looking for size, not quality. They told her not to wait that long to harvest. The food would taste better if she picked it before it reached complete maturity.

Mama lost interest in the contests and never entered again. She did take us to the annual 4-H parades. The parades consisted of our school and girls from other counties who dressed in white dresses with the green 4-H banner draped across their shoulders. They marched down the main street following the pitiful high school band.

Mama did learn a few things from the 4-H Demo Leaders. These ladies were paid to assist women on the farm and teach them how to improve country living. Mama already knew most of what they were teaching except how to make soda crackers. We preferred her biscuits anyway.

She was now busy keeping her house in order while Daddy and my brothers worked the farm. They utilized every inch of the land. Down the center of the farm was a natural fresh water spring. Daddy planted rice on both sides of the spring. He learned this somewhere while he was in the military, during World War I. They shared the harvested rice with the community; no other family had a spring that's needed to grow rice.

The main staples on the farm were cotton, peanuts, sugar cane, cows, hogs, string beans, greens, and corn that we planted for a food packing company. Daddy practiced the barter system for things we could not grow. We swapped eggs to get coffee and flour, apples to get cheese, sold sugar canes and peanuts to get cash for clothing. We picked cotton for larger farms to get canning jars and farming equipment and other household items.

These were hard times in many cities but our close-knit community felt little affect from the depression, because of their sharing practices. No one went hungry. The drought, rain or locusts hadn't affected our land.

We listened to the radio to hear about the nation's affairs. I could not imagine eating from garbage cans, sleeping in crowded camps or living like hobos. The camps were called 'Hooverville' after President Hoover. It seemed as though the whole world was in dismay.

Mama said, "God is looking over us because we live right."

Hog killing time arrived. This was almost a ritual; it took several men to perform the process. They divided the hog into portions and shared it with other families. When they killed their hogs, they would do the same thing. I hated when that time came. I had fed the hogs for a long time and listening to their slaughter just hurt my little heart. I would get under the bed and wait until it was over.

Syrup-making time was one of my favorite activities. It was like a weeklong party. We were the only family that had a syrup-making machine. The families that grew sugarcane would come to our house to get their syrup processed. They would give Daddy a portion of their syrup, which he would sell to larger stores in the city.

The day would start with the men stacking the cane stalks in a pile near the cane mill. The cane mill sat in the middle of the yard. We placed a large canister over the spout that caught the cane juice that would later be cooked into syrup. A leaver was attached to the cane mill and hooked to a mule that walked round and round, grinding the juice from the sugarcane. The next step was building a four-block foundation to hold the five by four foot galvanized pan that holds the juice over the fire.

Each man had a job, along with an assistant. One man

fed the cane stalks into the mill. Another took away the juiced shucks. Another person kept the fire burning evenly under the pan, and another skimmed the foam off the simmering syrup, placing it in wooded kegs. The foam-filled kegs were the start of corn liquor, moonshine and any other kind of spirits used to make a happy party.

After the syrup cooled, the women poured it into tin one-gallon buckets. They also served food on a long table that the men built just for this occasion. The adults planned each meal the day before by coordinating what each family could bring. I looked forward to the cookies and candy. The women made taffy from the syrup. The syrup simmered until it got thicker, then butter and flavoring were added. Then they would pull the candy back and forth until it cooled a little and stiffened. They would twist it into a braid, cool it completely and cut into small pieces.

When the crickets began chirping, the bats were flying low and the orange sun was almost gone, the big feast was over. Now it was time for socializing. Two bonfires were built, one for the men and one for the women. The children had to go inside where the older children would babysit. I snuck out.

After a few swigs of corn liquor, the men got very happy and a few of the women found everything funny too. I wanted to know what was so funny, so I hid behind the rose bush by the men and listened. None of the jokes were funny to me, except one a neighbor told.

'Ole Joe said, "Man, when I clamped down on that big titty, she let out a howl of sheer joy!"

Some of the men almost fell over laughing so hard.

I grabbed my flat chest and thought, that's not funny. I would have bashed his head in with a big rock.

31

I decided to crawl over to the women's section. They were laughing just as loud. My little seven-year-old body had no trouble hiding in the bushes.

One lady asked, "Ya'll hear about what happened to Lizzy?"

"No, child, when did she get back?"

"That fool been back. Wearin' a crazy wig." All the women laughed. "That heifer didn't get enough when they beat the hell outta her and took her to the Louisiana line and told her not to ever come back, or come anywhere near their husbands. It ain't been a year yet. She came back with the same old tricks. This time they beat her up and cut off both her ears... not one—both! Took her back to the Louisiana line and told her they will kill her if they ever see her black ass again!"

"Oh my, she is lucky they didn't kill her this time. Them white women ain't playin.'"

"That's what she gets for bein' a snobby whore."

Lizzy was a beautiful young lady that mysteriously showed up in the community after the oldest couple, in their late nineties, passed away. She claimed to be their granddaughter. She moved into their log cabin but wasn't very neighborly.

The whole community had totally cared for the old couple by giving food, wood clothing, medicine, and anything they needed. I liked going to the log cabin. They decorated the main room in such an odd way. The old lady would pull pages out of catalogs and paste them on the wall like wallpaper. The wood stove always had a black, iron teakettle sitting on it as though she was expecting company. They seemed so happy all the time. She always wore a bonnet, and he wore the same floppy, black hat.

32

They made everyone feel welcome. They never spoke of a granddaughter.

After that incident, Lizzy was never seen again. The log cabin finally rotted and fell to the ground.

The syrup season was over with enough syrup to last until the next season, and Daddy reaped a good profit in merchandise and plenty of syrup for the family.

We were all early risers and Mama always fed us a hearty breakfast. The smell of bacon, fresh baked biscuits and coffee brewing filled the air; there were no late sleepers. Even the crowing roosters couldn't catch us sleeping, except on rainy days. There were no alarm clocks and no one summoned us from a sound sleep, we just automatically got up.

Mama made me a beautiful blue flowered dress for my first day of school. It was gathered at the waist, with a big bow tied in the back. I was as happy as a six year old could be. She combed my hair into five big plaits sticking out like Pippi Longstocking.

Daddy went into the city to purchase my first schoolbook, See Spot Run. My siblings before me used the same book and I memorized it. I now wonder why they even called it a book—it was just a small pamphlet. My eight siblings were not as fortunate. They had to wait a week to get their books because all the new books had been sent to the white schools and their old books had to be stamped "Negros only" never to be returned. Some of the pages were missing, writing scribbles throughout and some looked almost destroyed.

"All right children, take your seats at your table," Miss Essie said. She passed a plain sheet of paper to each of us. "Write or draw anything you want. I will come back to pick them up."

Daddy was the writer in our house. He finished elementary school in Louisiana, which qualified him as an educated man, especially for a black man. His penmanship was surprising to many because he wrote italic style. He became a spokesman for the black community and secretary for the school and church. He never told us where he learned to write like that. It was very impressive. I always felt, the person who taught him made him promise not to tell. I took my piece of paper and made scratches on each line. I thought it looked just like Daddy's handwriting.

I felt so special that day. Grades one through eight met together in the same room used as a Baptist Church on Sunday. I was the smallest child in class. Someone made me a chair out of a wooden apple cart. They removed one end of the cart, placed it in the middle and painted it green. Miss Essie set my chair next to her desk, which earned me the name 'teacher's pet' from that day on.

The weather changed. The wind howled like a fat pig stuck in a hole and it was cold as an ice cube. The final harvesting was underway. Crystal and I prepared to pick the 'peanut tree.' It wasn't really a tree. Daddy would stake a five-foot pole into the ground. The peanuts were pulled out of the ground and stacked around the pole with the peanuts facing outward. After the stack dried, Crystal and I would spend every evening after school filling Croaker sacks with peanuts. We had many fun peanut fights. Throwing the peanuts at each other broke the boredom. The peanuts would then be stored in the barn.

When empty, we used the Croaker sacks to gather firewood for the wood heater. Pine knots had a certain amount of oil substance that could start the oak to burn.

The knots were hard to find, and Crystal and I would search for hours. We might only find five or six but we kept looking until we filled the bin with enough for the entire winter.

Mama would stink up the kitchen making her famous soap. She used the leftover fat meat 'grease'; clarified it by heating it and straining it through cheesecloth. She added lye while it was still hot and mixed it to a smooth paste. When it cooled, she cut it into bars. That stuff would get the dirt out of anything.

The men were busy getting a good supply of wood for the winter and repairing the leaky barns. Now everything was ready for winter.

Christmas was just around the corner. The smell of holly berries and rum soaked fruitcakes were in the air. Mama started her fruitcakes early. She would steam the cakes to perfection in a pressure cooker. Then she wrapped them in cloth and poured rum over them periodically until Christmas Day.

Daddy and the boys killed a hog, mainly to get a ham for Christmas day. My sisters and I picked up empty cigarette boxes by the highway to get the red opening strip to decorate the Christmas tree. We popped popcorn and strung it on thread using a needle to create a chain that wind in layers around the tree.

A few days before Christmas, Daddy and Mama would hitch a ride into town with anyone that might pick them up. Surely, someone in the community would come by before long. My sisters and I knew exactly what we would get...a ten-cent naked, bald headed doll. My brothers would get slingshots or marbles. Everyone would get a whole orange, a whole banana, candy and a variety of nuts

35

in real stockings that Mama had saved for the occasion. I never saw Mama and Daddy exchange gifts, not even on their birthdays.

There was such a spirit of Christmas in the air. My brothers and sisters and I were all on our best behavior. We knew Santa would be watching our every move. We were fortunate enough to have a radio and the Christmas carols would blast through the house. Daddy and the boys made sure to cut plenty of wood for the heater and the kitchen stove. Mama and us girls baked cakes. There were always at least seven cakes besides the fruitcakes.

On Christmas day, the house had to be in tiptop shape to welcome any visitor who might drop by to express season's greetings and exchange a small plate of food, the ritual repeated until every house had been visited. Daddy or Mama would make the rounds then place the collected food on the dinner table with all the other festive food.

We all had high spirits on Christmas and Crystal and I were always the first to rush to the Christmas tree. Fruit, candy and nut-filled stockings hung on a nail near the tree. Mama made the final preparations. She put the ham in the oven, stuffed a hen with cornbread dressing, and candied the sweet potatoes. The night before, she cooked the macaroni and cheese. The cakes, pies and pudding were prepared almost a week before. Potato salad was the only vegetable on the menu. Every person in the house stuffed themselves with the rich foods.

The festive day finally slipped away. The following day, Crystal and I made dresses for our dolls. There was no shortage of scrap material. Mama would go to the garment factory in the city and ask for throwaway scraps. When some of the ladies found out, that Mama had nine children, they would save big bags of scrap flannel and sneak whole bolts of material in the center of the bags. She made shirts and long legged underwear for all of us.

The weather got so cold, we only went outside when necessary—to school and church. We played games inside. My sister Crystal and I would play jacks using rocks. She won most of the time. I was sure it was because her hands were larger than mine and I could not flip the rocks very well. Tic-Tac-Toe was another favorite game. Mama roasted peanuts and gave each of us a big handful as an after dinner snack.

The cold days lasted until about April. Hibernation ended and spring-cleaning began. Everyone took part in the annual ritual. Mama would be the director and everyone followed orders. The girls took all the blankets off the beds and threw them across the fences, hedges or anything that could hold them up. The boys took the mattresses and placed them on a grassy spot. Daddy and the boys took the bedsprings, and placed them on the naked ground and poured kerosene over them and set them afire to kill any bed bugs hiding on them. Then they walked to the riverbanks to get white sand. We spread it on the floor to cleanse the wood as we walked. After about two weeks of walking on the sandy floor, we swept and mopped it to an almost white finish.

All the curtains were pulled down, washed, put in a big pot of boiling water and re-hung until next spring. The iron cooking pots were set out on the ground, doused with kerosene and burned to remove the old baked on food. Crystal and I cleaned the shelves and threw away any old, unusable stuff. Maxine had a knack for sewing. She was busy repairing clothing and any torn items that needed mending. She knew how to use Mama's Singer Sewing Machine.

Daddy was busy getting all the farm tools ready. He learned to file and sharpen saws and plows while in the Civil Conservation Camp. We made extra money by helping other farmers plant their crops.

A neighbor asked Daddy to let me drop fertilizer as he plowed his field. My cousin warned me to watch out for him. He had raped her and really hurt her because of the size of his penis. She was married and had never seen one that large. Daddy didn't know this; we could not talk about such things with adults. This neighbor told Daddy he wanted me to help because I was a fast worker. Daddy sent me to help.

We had been working about an hour when he said, "I want to give you a present. A gold watch would look good on you."

My heart raced with fear. I was only ten years old and had never had sex before. I feared he would kill me trying.

"Now don't be scared. When you get to the end of the row, just go out in those trees. Nobody can see and I will come out there and make you feel real good," he said.

My heart was pumping far too fast. My only hope was that his wife was in the house and could hear my screams. Every time we got near the end of the row, he told me to go in the woods. He kept plowing the mules near me. I never said one word to him. When I finished the last row, I did not wait to get paid. I dropped my bucket and ran home as fast as I could.

After that day, I avoided him. When he spoke in church as a deacon on Sunday, I would always look away. I felt creepy whenever he came near me.

A few weeks later, I was almost raped again. One day on my way home from school, a man in a big gravel truck attempted to rape me. Our school was located half a mile across the railroad track through a swamp that was full of snakes and thick marshland. Big logs lined the open path allowing us to travel to and from school using the shortcut. Heavy rains would flood the shortcut so bad that we could not see the logs. Then we would have to take the longer route home, almost a mile in distance along the highway.

This day I remained behind at school to help the teacher grade her papers. She had only completed the eighth grade herself. I liked helping her. She was the only teacher for all the grades first through eighth.

I walked along the highway on the way home. A big gravel truck pulled up beside me. A big white man spit a mouthful of tobacco out the window.

He said in a loud voice, "Hey, nigger how about a piece of pussy? I got two dollars."

My feet took off like a jet plane and my heart raced like drums. I knew to stay on the highway. Going to the woods would have been unwise.

He laughed in a sinister voice. "Ha ha ha ha! You had better stop gal! I mean it! Stop, I said!"

I continued to run. He stayed right beside me until we got in sight of my house. Laughing, he sped up the truck and drove off. I was panting and blowing when I fell on our porch.

That night I had nightmares. I could hear his laughter and it woke me up. I did not tell a soul about the incident until I was an adult and had children of my own.

Summer came; the farm was in full bloom and the heat waves had no mercy. In order to endure the heat our day began before the mighty sun arrived. We worked until about 11:00, had dinner, rest a few hours then go back and work until sundown when the bats came flying out, swooping down toward our heads. Then we fed the cattle and put them away.

Supper was served. I was assigned to the kitchen to prepare the meals. I could not go out in the sun or get in the dew. My eyes would swell shut from the sun and the dew gave me big welts where it touched me. But no one lives on a farm and doesn't work.

Mama taught me to pull a chair up to the stove and cook greens, peas, cornbread and bake sweet potatoes. We would clean the house and prepare the food to be cooked the next day.

World War II was raging. My brother George had already been drafted and was serving the country. Lee was excited because he had been drafted and was waiting to be called to duty.

I thought Lee was such a kind and gentle soul. He had a learning disability so he hated school. None of the "stuff" made sense to him and he was ashamed that he could not do any of his schoolwork. He asked Mama to let him drop out of school and go to work to help the family. She realized he was struggling in school and allowed him to drop out because she didn't know how to help him.

He got a job on the farm next to ours. The owner was not very nice. Lee worked from sun up to sun down for six dollars a week. Mama would look over and see him plowing in the blazing hot sun and cry. Lee would give her five dollars and keep one for himself so he could go to the movies and by a hamburger and soda pop.

Lee would be leaving to go to the army in just a few

40

weeks. He gave me his bicycle, which was too large for me. He attempted to teach me how to ride it but I could never apply the brakes soon enough. Hitting something was the only way I could stop. I still carry some of the scars from that bike.

It was a cool October evening and the sun had just gone down. Lee had just taken a spin on his bicycle before retiring for the evening. We were taking chairs inside from the porch. The coolness and darkness had taken its place when suddenly a loud scraping car, brake-screeching sound filled the air. A car stopped and the driver was screaming and waving at another motorist that sped by and completely ignored him. A second car stopped.

It was too dark to see what was going on but we heard him say, "Please help me, help me! I just hit a boy on a bicycle!"

We all just knew it was Lee.

"Help me get him to the nearest hospital," the man said.

Every one of us ran to the highway a few yards away. Daddy was the first to reach the scene. He asked someone in the crowd to stop Mama from getting to close to Lee. Someone sent all the children back into the house. Daddy confirmed it was Lee and went with him to the hospital. The driver that hit him took them to the hospital seven miles away.

The house filled with neighbors waiting to hear the outcome of Lee's accident. Daddy returned with a sad look on his face. Mama cried louder. He had not explained anything at this point; he tried to calm her down first.

He said, "Lee didn't feel anything it was so instant. The impact didn't give him time to feel anything. It seemed as though Lee was getting out of the way of a Greyhound bus when he rode his bike into the path of the car. It was traveling 80 miles an hour."

Daddy went on to explain that the driver was on his way to Jackson Mississippi Airport. He was returning to Germany to do some type of business for the military. He told Daddy that he had insurance; he gave Daddy all the information needed for compensation for his loss.

A shyster lawyer told Daddy he needed a lawyer to represent him in order to get all his benefits. The lawyer cheated Daddy out of most of his money. He never did know the total amount the insurance paid out. The lawyer took his deduction, giving Daddy a check for $1800.00. There was nothing Daddy could do. He was the only lawyer in town.

Mama continued to grieve for Lee; she blamed herself for his death.

"If I had not allowed him to drop out of school he might still be alive."

She would sit on the front porch until late in the night as if she was waiting for him to come home. After Lee's death, she was never the same.

The war was over now and Calvin graduated from elementary school. The nearest high school for Negro's was seven miles away. The school bus was not allowed to pick us up even though we paid annual taxes on our land that helped pay for the bus.

Most of the riders were sharecropper's kids. I remember the white kids laughing out the bus windows and saying, "Hey, nigger. Aren't you cold?"

I would say, "Kiss my ass." Of course, they could not hear me.

In order to get to our high school, we had to pay twenty cents to ride the Greyhound bus to and from school. My first year in high school was Calvin's senior year.

After graduation, he decided to join the Navy. That meant I would have to travel to the city by myself for school. Mama was afraid for me to be alone in the city for almost four hours after school waiting for the bus. School got out at 3:00 and the Greyhound didn't leave the station until 6:45.

I had already learned to do my own hair. Mama broke so many combs on my hair because it was so very thick. She could not comb it without hurting me so I learned to do it on my own. I taught myself to braid in the field using the tall grass as hair. I would start a French braid in one row of grass and make a braid a quarter mile long. When Daddy was plowing the fields, it really vexed him to plow through my braids.

When corn matured to the silk stage, I would style the silk of corn in many different styles. This was the beginning of my desire to be a beautician. It was the easiest, rewarding and most fun thing I had ever done.

Mama found a beautician in the city that had a little beauty shop in her home next to the school I was attending. She told the owner that I had too much time to waste waiting for the bus and she was afraid I would get into trouble. She told the owner that if she would teach me for one hour I would clean up for one hour. She told her I liked doing hair and would be easy to teach. The owner agreed and I spent the school year under her supervision.

When school was out for the summer, oh how I missed that little shop. I had become the only beautician in my neighborhood. I was a proud kid with a good income. I

43

kept some of my money and gave the balance to Mama.

She would say, "Sessy, you bought this coffee," or whatever it was she had purchased for the house. "I am glad you did that. You did good."

This was such a boost to hear these words from her. It made me glow with such pride and I awaited that loving stroke on my cheek with the back of her hand. That was a good day.

There was much to be done on the farm, but I was looking forward to going back to school. I panicked when I learned that the Greyhound workers had gone on strike. How would I get to school? My dream of becoming a schoolteacher was fleeting at an alarming speed.

I thought about my friends who had dropped out of school, had babies and gotten fat. They were content with their lives. I became fearful that I would follow their example. However, I had greater aspirations and maintained a bit of hope that I would not be caught up in the same mediocrities.

Being the only beautician in the neighborhood, I expressed my disappointment about the bus strike to everyone who sat in my chair. They would get an earful of my whining about not being able to go to school.

Ms. Green, a teacher at an underprivileged school for black children, came to me to get her hair done. She listened to my story and decided to help me. She told Mama that she could get me enrolled in the school where she worked if Mama would let me go. The school was thirty miles away and I would reside in a girl's dormitory.

I knew Mama would agree. She had always encouraged me to get an education. She told Ms. Green that I was a good cook and that would help pay most of my tuition.

School would start in three months and there was a lot of work to do on the farm before then. Crystal, Larry and I were the oldest kids left at home. Lyn and Dean were too young to do much of anything.

A change came over the whole community that summer. A blanket of fear fell over every household because of the murders.

Childhood Memories

They shall abundantly utter the memory of thy
great goodness, and shall sing of thy righteousness.

Psalms 145:7

Chapter 4
My Dark Teen Summer

This summer held so many feelings, sorrow, fear and the struggle to find my place in the world. At sixteen, I no longer felt like a child. The world rested on my shoulders. I became a woman; there was nothing childish about me. Or so I thought.

Our family changed. Maxine, my oldest sister, got pregnant and dropped out of school. This broke Mama's heart. Maxine moved to Louisiana to live with Mama's sister. Our community considered her an outcast, having a child out of wedlock.

Calvin, my brother above me, finished high school and joined the Navy. Calvin was my hero. I looked up to him. I thought he must be the smartest boy in my high school. He got good grades, played football, and graduated class valedictorian. He proved to be as smart as I always thought. He was the only one of us to have hair like Mama's. He would wet it and put 'grease' on it and it would fall into waves.

He was also the miser of the family. If he made a dollar, he saved fifty cents. Every time the rain was pouring down outside, he paced the floor waiting for it to stop so he could look for his money stash that he buried in the ground. He feared it would wash away. We tried to find his treasure but

47

we never caught him digging it up or stashing it. He almost never wrote home after he joined the Navy and we missed him.

Larry, my younger brother, got a summer job at a fishing factory in Gulfport Mississippi. He bought an old car to get around in the city. He had never been away from home and Mama worried about him.

Daddy got a message that Larry was in jail in Gulfport. Daddy never learned to drive a car, so he got a neighbor to drive him to Gulfport to rescue Larry and find out what on earth he had done to get thrown in jail. Larry had not committed a crime. His co-worker was a criminal who took advantage of his country innocence. The co-worker asked Larry to give him a ride home. Larry agreed, not knowing the items he put in the back of his car were stolen goods. The police stopped them and searched the car. Finding the items, they arrested Larry. The co-worker denied putting them in his trunk. Larry lost his job and returned home. He then enlisted in the military.

My cousin, Shant, was a twenty-eight year old, well built, very handsome, intelligent black man. He had become an accomplished cabinetmaker while in the military. He served most of his duty in Italy where he learned to speak Italian quite well.

Shant was hired to build kitchen cabinets in the home of a factory worker, who was an employee at the new "white only" factory. The workers wife came from Italy. He met her while stationed there in the military.

The iceman was delivering ice to the house where Shant was working. He said he looked through the bedroom window and saw Shant and the factory workers wife in bed making love.

48

He watched as they made passionate love, their naked bodies becoming one. Shant lifted her up into his muscular arms. She wrapped her long silky legs around his waist, locking her feet together and resting them on his curvaceous buttocks. He held her tiny, beautiful, ivory colored body close with one arm using the other hand to gently enter her. She threw her head back, closing her eyes and moaning in ecstasy.

After watching the pair for an hour, he rushed to the factory to tell the husband what he had just witnessed. They shut down the factory immediately and most of the men jumped in the back of open-bed trucks in search of Shant.

"Let's kill that nigger."

"We gonna hang that son-of-a-bitch from a tree and let his dick hang in the burning sun."

Shouts like these were heard as they drove through town. Word spread like wildfire. Before nightfall, every household knew of the scandalous rumor. Even though it was a hot summer evening, no one went out to sit on his or her porches that night. Mama told us to stay away from the windows. We spoke in whispers, as though outsiders were listening.

Daddy found out that the drunken men had ransacked Shant's mother's house looking for him but he had already fled to the woods.

Fear ruled the community and only the sound of crickets pierced the night. The fireflies flickered in the pitch-black darkness.

Men using flashlights, searched through the trees and bushes shooting at anything that moved. They decided to go home and continue the search at daybreak.

Shant's body was found the next evening in a shallow hole he had dug himself. He lay down and covered himself with branches and leaves to hide from the angry mob. He eventually died there from gunshot wounds.

After Shant's murder, the workers' wife was never seen again. The husband said she decided to go back to Italy. No one knew for sure, but most felt she met the same fate as Shant. No one investigated or even made a report about Shant's death or the missing wife.

When things got back to normal, Mama gave Crystal and me permission to start going back to the movies on Saturdays. We could only see Tarzan, cartoons and cowboy movies. There were times when some of the kids didn't have the ten-cent fare for the movies. We would wait until all the kids arrived and help sneak them inside. We would all bunch up around the ticket area and distract the agent, then two of us handed him the ten cents at the same time. The broke kid then ran like hell to get inside.

After the movie, we indulged in a delicious, greasy, ten-cent hamburger and washed it down with a nickel soda pop. We all had to get home before the sun set. Oh, yes, those were the good old days! We spent many Saturday evenings doing the Tarzan yell or acting like the characters we had just seen on the big screen.

We had to get our clothes ready for church before going to bed. Although Daddy believed in God, he did not go to church with the rest of us. Church was a must in our house. If any of the kids missed church, we could not go to the Sunday evening dance party that old man Tom provided at his grocery store.

He cleared the floor, pushed the kegs aside and hooked up the jukebox that played both black and white music.

Whatever side put the nickel in first is what we danced to. The room was integrated and we all danced together like old friends, as though color didn't exist. After the last dance, we walked out separately, not speaking a word to one another.

I was thinking about school again, which was only a couple of months away. I felt bad leaving Crystal behind. She was my closest friend and we did everything together. I worried about her. Who would do her hair? Mama's hair was long and straight. She really didn't know how to comb thick, kinky hair like ours.

I needed clothes for school, so mama let me visit my Aunt in Louisiana. She got me a job washing dishes in the restaurant next to where she worked.

Summer had almost ended when another terrible incident occurred in our community. About a year before, a sixteen-year-old runaway boy, named Willie came to our community. A milk dairy owner took him in, in exchange for a place to stay and a little change to go to the movies.

Everyone accepted Willie. He even joined our church and would sometimes go to the movies with us. The dairy owner had a nineteen-year-old daughter that would sneak out of the house at night to sleep with Willie. Her father confronted her and Willie after catching them in the act of making love. He became irate with both of them until she said that Willie had forced her to have sex with him. The following day, Willie was found hanging from the loft in the barn. We had no way to inform his relatives of his death. He never spoke of his family or where they were from.

The community raised money to bury Willie, and we held his funeral at our church.

51

The farmer had the mitigated gall to attend the funeral and speak on how sorry he was. "Willie was a good ol' boy. It's too bad he hung himself playing cowboys and Indians, like he saw in the movies."

Of course, Willie's hanging never was reported, not in the newspaper or on the radio.

During my final week home, before leaving for school, I started to have mixed feelings about leaving. I had never been that far from home. School was thirty-five miles away. I did feel blessed to be able to pursue my dreams but I still felt my family needed me.

Our church presented a program celebrating the end of summer and everyone attended. It was a pleasant dark night and we could see the stars and the big dipper shining in the sky. The air felt a bit sticky from the summer heat. We were walking home. My sister, Crystal, and Larry and Dean, my brothers, were not too far behind Mama and Daddy. Bringing up the rear were John and I, an older boy who was always asking me for a date. John was a bit taller than me, about five-feet three inches tall and ugly as hell. His skin was dark as night and he had terrible acne. To make matters worse, he had bad breath. He grabbed my shoulder and tried to kiss me.

I raised my voice and said, "Hey stop that before I call my Daddy."

"Oh, don't do that. Come on you might like it. It's just a kiss," he said.

While his mouth was over my mouth, he rubbed my vagina. When I pushed him, he pushed me to the ground, lifted my dress, grabbed my panties at the crotch and pulled them to one side trying to enter me. His penis felt like a stick of wood.

To avoid anyone hearing me, I clenched my teeth in anger and fear and growled, "Stop."

I jolted my hips from side to side, but he kept trying to force himself inside me. I kept moving as if I was doing a hula dance. He finally gave up and ran away. I laid there for a moment until I heard footsteps approaching. I jumped up, out of breath.

Crystal asked, "What's wrong with you?

"Nothing," I said.

I went home still a virgin and never spoke a word of what happened to me that night.

My Dark Teen Summer

I was dumb with silence, I held my peace,
even from good; and my sorrow was stirred.

Psalms 39:2

Chapter 5
Growing Up At School

On Monday, I would start my first day of school at Prentiss Normal Industrial Institute in Prentiss Mississippi. Mama searched the house trying to find something to pack the few clothes I had. She did not have any luggage, not even a large paper bag. She found and old, faded out, beat up medical doctor's bag that originally had a handle on each side, but one handle was broken. She asked Daddy to fix it with the wire he used to fix our tattered shoes. She also found a pair of boots she thought would be useful in case it snowed, but the boots looked horrible. I didn't know that at the time because I had nothing to compare them to. They were similar to the ones that Miss Kitty on Gun Smoke had thrown away. I took the medical bag and my lace up boots and waited for the teacher to pick me up.

I tried with all my might to fight back the tears. I thought, I am only fifteen years old and have to face the world like a big girl.

Mama doled out her motherly advice. "Sessy, you be a good girl and keep your dress down."

"Yes, Mama, I will." If she only knew how many times, I had defended that little spot.

Miss Green's car pulled up. She and Mama talked about my well-being and when Mama would see me again. "I will bring her back for Christmas break. She should write you and let you know how she is doing. Don't worry, I will look after her," she told Mama.

Leaving Crystal behind was the hardest thing I've ever had to do, but I sucked it up. I watched the house until it was out of sight. The scenic ride on Highway 35N was breath taking. The big farms with the white picket fences seemed unreal to me. I had never seen such large houses and beautifully landscaped yards. The trip took about an hour and a half.

The campus surprised me. I wasn't sure of what to expect. The dormitory was two stories high and there were so many other buildings surrounding it.

Miss Green took me to the office to help me check in and find my room assignment. The lady behind the desk wasn't friendly at all. She was big, fat, and dark. She wore a dress that looked two sizes too small. I wondered why she had her hair in five braids. Braids were for kids. Even I had outgrown braids.

She completed the forms and said, "Follow me gal." She was very country, frumpy and didn't seem as though she should be working at a school.

The room she took me to was nice and clean. There were two bunks beds, four nightstands and two long study desks. It was the first time that I had a bed all to myself and I smiled.

All the students were asked to meet in the dining room at five o'clock to get acquainted with each other. Two of my roommates were like me, very country. The third was tall with a light complexion. She was a tough girl from the ghetto of Chicago. This was her second year on campus and she had made a name for herself. Her real name was

Yvonne but everyone called her 'Miss Big Bad Chicago'. I avoided her as much as I could.

One day, Yvonne lost her English book and she asked if she could borrow mine.

"Sure," I said, "just as soon as I finish my assignment."

She waited a little while and then came over to me, snatched my book and said, "Gimme this book. You should be finished by now."

The room turned dark and I could smell the anger in my nose. I jumped up and snatched the book out of her hand. Using both of mine, I smacked her in the face with it. Her nose ran with blood and her right eye swelled shut. I dragged her to the stairs to throw her down, but my other roommates grabbed me pulling me off her. They took her back to our room and cleaned her up. She never bullied me again. In fact, she acted as if it never happened.

When people asked what happened to her face, she said, "I fell down the stairs."

My life on campus got better. I found my niche. A niche I never knew existed. My day started in the morning. I cooked the same breakfast I made at home, just in bigger pots. Soon, I became head cook. I had no trouble preparing the big dishpan of grits, slicing whole sticks of bologna, and making salmon gravy for the grits. The staff was surprised that a fifteen year old could cook grits without lumps. Many of the staff decided to eat breakfast in our dining room for the first time.

Some of the school rules were a bit strange to me. We were allowed to go to the movies. The school bus carried us downtown. The boys sat on one side of the bus, the girls on the other. The girls were marched to their seats on the opposite side of the theater from the boys. I had never been

57

involved in so many activities. Life was good. I became a cheerleader for the football team and traveled with the team to most of the games.

I made a little money pressing and curling hair in my room when the staff was not looking. I used the barter system with girls who had no money. I accepted twenty five sheets of lined writing paper for a hot curl, five pencils or clothing I could wear, anything that added up to fifty cents or a dollar.

The mean Matron that checked me in the first day was the main one that I feared would catch me working. However, it wasn't long before I fixed most of the staff's hair. One of the teachers recognized my fear of getting caught. She decided to help me.

She told the Matron, "Girl, you got nice long hair. If you got it pressed and let it flow you would be a knockout."

"But I don't know anybody who can do it. The white shops will not take us and I can't do it myself."

"How does my hair look?" the teacher asked.

"Your hair always looks good."

The teacher leaned in close and said, "I will tell you who does mine if you can keep it a secret.

"I will. I will."

"In order to not implicate her, she can only do it in your room on a hot plate. It's Sessy. She can fix some hair. Girl, in just a few minutes she can whip you up to look great. Sessy helps a lot of us with our hair. I'll ask her if she could do yours."

"Oh, please ask her and I will not report her," the Matron said.

The first time I worked on the Matrons hair I felt like I was working on a bulldog or a pit bull, just waiting to snap at me any minute. She did not say a word to me. I was very cautious not to burn her scalp. I just knew she would grab the hot comb out of my hand and beat the hell out of me.

I must admit, the Matron looked like a different person from under those plaits. I think she gained a new attitude. She even smiled every now and then. A one hundred percent improvement in her appearance.

Most of the girls in my dorm snuck out to meet boyfriends. Not me. I was too busy to think about sneaking out for any reason. Although one of the older guys had been making passes at me. I just pretended I didn't understand what he meant. He attended the adult section on campus studying to become a tailor. I was not attracted to him at all.

I was having trouble getting rides home for school breaks. I learned the student that was trying to date me lived not too many miles from where I lived. His name was Alvin, but he called himself Al. He suggested that we share the same ride and I accepted. We stopped by his parent's house first. His father decided to ride with us.

When we arrived at my parents house, his father shouted, "Jim is that you?"

They embraced like old friends, "Henry, is that you? I thought I would never see you again."

They told us how they met so many years ago when they were young men working in the turpentine fields. "This is my daughter Sessy," Daddy said.

Henry introduced his son Alvin. Daddy and Henry spent the whole evening talking about old times.

The summer was hot, as usual. So many things on the farm had changed. They were doing less farming. In fact, the government was paying farmers not to plant certain products.

Crystal dated a boy she met at the new high school. It was built for Black kids and a school bus had been provided. They built it so far back in the woods, it took a vehicle to get there.

My feelings about the farm had changed. Our house had been modernized but the farm seemed to be neglected. Mama was not feeling well most of the time and Daddy just let things go to pot. I spent a lot of time trying to get the house up to par. I made new curtains and helped Mama in her smaller garden. I fixed things that were broken and planted a new flower garden. I worked so hard that summer that I lost two dress sizes.

Mama and Daddy did not get along very well. There was tension between them. Mama confided in me that she was thinking about leaving Daddy because of his 'running around' as she called it. "If he leaves, you may have to come home," she said.

She continued to talk, but my mind stuck on the possibility of leaving my beloved school. School was my life. A beautiful life.

Al's parents and mine got together often. After returning to school, we secretly started dating. It was what I would call a platonic relationship. I could only see him in the dining room at mealtime or on trips with the football team. He was a chaperone on the bus and his classes were on the other side of the campus.

We would write notes to each other. I really didn't know how to write a love note, I just answered his questions and left it alone. How could I express something that I did not feel?

My trips home were not that exciting anymore. Mama

and Daddy did not separate but it was not a happy marriage. It felt like a cold war.

I did not want to spend another whole summer at home, so I asked Mama to let me go to summer school. She agreed and was happy to know that I wanted to continue school. She felt that the more days I spent in school the sooner I would become a teacher.

I experienced a wonderful summer on campus that year. Most of the students went home. All of them were glad to get the summer break from school. My roommates took off the day after the semester ended. That left me with the whole room to myself. That was the first time in my fifteen years that I ever slept in a room all by myself.

The adults treated me like staff and it felt so good. The staff put me in complete charge of the kitchen meal-planning, inventory, cleaning and delegating. I joined the choir at church. Some of the teachers took me to the movies or on shopping trips. It was one of the best laid-back summers of my life.

Everything must come to an end. The kids and staff returned to school. I took part in helping the new kids find their rooms and anything else that I could do.

I was glad to see my roommates and they were glad to see me. Al made it back and I was glad to see him also. He brought me up on the gossip from home. It was the same old stuff that was going on when I left the farm.

Choosing to stay on campus turned out to be the best choice after all.

Growing up at School

A wise man will hear, and will increase learning; and
a man of understanding shall attain unto wise counsels:

Proverbs 1:5

Chapter 6
Marriage for Sessy

Al and I grew closer. We saw each other at meal times. One night I confided in him. "Mama and Daddy haven't been getting along. Mama is thinking about leaving Daddy. If she does, I will have to leave school 'cause Mama won't be able to pay my tuition."

"But you work so hard. Don't you pay most of your tuition?"

"Well, yes. But Mama still has to pay a portion of it. She sells things from around the farm to pay her share. Eggs, chickens, fruits and vegetables, peanuts...you get the idea. Without her contribution, I'll have to leave school. I don't know what to do. There is no way I am going to give up on my dream. Mama says, 'where there's a will there's a way'. I just have to find the way."

The next morning, Al and I met in the dining room for our usual breakfast together.

"Sessy," he said. "I have an answer to your problem. If they cannot pay your tuition, then I will. I get a G.I. Bill check every month. I can pay it out of that. We could get married—"

"You know we can't get married," I said, holding up my hands. "I'm just sixteen."

"One of my friends is a minister. I can secure a marriage

license and he can perform the ceremony in his home. No one needs to know until after you get to be eighteen," he said.

It did not fit well in my gut but it was a way out. I told him I would think about it. Do people get married when they are not in love? It seemed I had found 'a way' after all. I decided to accept his offer, reinforcing the fact that he would pay my tuition. Our next trip home we were married. I felt so guilty for not telling Mama.

We had not consummated our marriage yet. It never entered my mind that I would lose my virginity so young. I had counted on waiting until I was eighteen years old. We continued with our regular routine as usual. I returned to the girls' dorm and he went back to the male quarters where he resided.

The time came to pay my tuition. The school had this appalling practice of identifying who lagged in their payments. They called the late people up on stage in front of the assembly. I had been called up before. This time, I set snuggly in my seat smiling, knowing that my name would not be called.

"Sessy Pierson." What? I tried to locate Al in the audience as I walked up to the stage. I found him in the crowd and hoped he would correct the mistake. He did not move one inch. We were lined up and reprimanded for not paying our share like everyone else.

When it was over, I rushed to Al, "Why didn't you pay like you promised?"

"I was going to pay, but if I had they would find out we were married. You know we are trying to keep it a secret." That was his answer and I was too dumb to tell him he could have given me the money and I could pay to protect

64

our secret. I had never heard of an annulment.

I went to the President's office and negotiated with him to allow me to do more work so I could cover all my tuition. He agreed and I was given the job to tutor at the elementary campus. I like helping the struggling kids learn new things. It also made me feel like I was already a teacher.

One stormy day I was rushing back to the dorm, trying not to get drenched. Al saw me and gave me his hat to keep my hair from getting wet. When I reached the dorm, Matron saw me wearing his hat and threw a fit.

"What do you mean wearing a man's hat? You know that's against the rules. You will be punished for that. Three days out of school, starting tomorrow. That will cool your little tail down. Believe me you will work every minute miss sassy."

The next morning, right after breakfast, Matron took me into the pantry where she had laid out half a hog on the butcher block for me to cut up and pack away. I took my own time cutting the meat so that I would not get finished too fast and be given another nasty job.

The next morning, she had another horrible job waiting for me.

She asked, "Do you have a pair of gloves?"

"No ma'am," I said.

"Then go back and put on a long sleeve shirt and hat, since you want to be the hat lady."

She was waiting at the back door when I returned. I followed her outside where she gave me a five-gallon bucket and walked me to the okra field. I knew I was in big trouble. The fuzz on the okra can make you itch like crazy.

She pointed to a large empty tub on the ground and said, "Don't stop until this tub is full."

Oh how I wanted to stab her, right in her big fat butt with the knife she had handed me to cut the okra. I was doing her job while I was supposed to be in class. That heifer is getting away with working the hell out of me.

News got around that she was mistreating me for a minor offense. Even the staff disagreed with her. One teacher informed me that I could return to her class whenever I wanted.

My roommates decided to sneak me out of the dorm and help me attend class. We made it to my first class. Just as I was settling in and getting warm greetings from my classmates, this big burly woman stormed through the door. It was Matron. She scanned the room looking for me. It was too late to duck down.

She found me and snarled my name. "Sessy, come out and I mean come out now."

I shuffled my little embarrassed butt toward her. I waited for the teacher to defend me but she didn't say one word. I wondered if she was as afraid of Matron as I.

Matron stomped her big butt in front of me not saying a word. She glanced back to see if I still followed her. She stepped inside the dorm door and turned on me. "You stupid girl. This could have been your last day. No, little missy, you broke the rules again. Just for that, you will get two days added. Try that again and you will get a whole week next time."

She took me outside and instructed me to rake the leaves on the big campus lawn. She had me start near the dorm and rake outward, which would put me near the street when the kids got out of school. Kids can be cruel. I tried to ignore them when they poked fun at me by saying idiotic things, such as—

"Hey Sessy, what did you do, kill your roommates?"

"How much time did you get?"

Did Matron forget I am her beautician? I could visualize her next appointment. I could get the straightening comb too hot and accidentally drop it down her back and watch her dance while the hot comb leaves its marks on her back. Or, I could fake a faint, lay the hot comb on her face, and let it fry for a while. But only if I want a death sentence.

Al heard about what she was doing to me and exploded. He went to the President's office and told him, "This shit has to quit. Sessy is my wife. Here is our marriage license. She will not rake another leaf."

After the President gave us a tongue-lashing for being so foolish, he accepted the marriage as legal. We were assigned a housing unit near the teachers' quarters.

My first night with my husband was disappointing. I heard other girls talking about what a thrill it was having sex. There had to be something wrong with me because I could find nothing good about it. Dealing with the bloody sheets was sickening. The girls forgot to tell me about that.

The next day was horrible. I had to go to class feeling sore and embarrassed. I walked with my head down. I felt like all eyes were on me, knowing what I had done last night. I felt dumb because I had no knowledge of how to have sex. I must be doing it wrong. Al did not try to introduce me to what I needed to know either.

Al graduated that year. He was now a certified tailor. We took our first trip home as a married couple. I feared telling Mama that I was married. Her reaction was much worse than I could have imagined.

She broke down and cried, "Oh, Sessy. Why Sessy? I wanted you to go to college." She ran outside to the back yard and screamed, shaking her head in disbelief. She reacted as if I had died. Of course, she was hurt. This twenty-seven year old man had stolen her child. She did not have a clue of how to save me from what she knew would later befall me.

Al got his first job teaching at a vocational school located in Jackson, Mississippi. He liked his job. I enrolled in school and completed the twelfth grade. I wanted to go to college and become a teacher. The college I wanted to attend was too far away. I could not stand sitting home doing nothing.

Al, and one of his friends, decided to form a partnership and open a 'Mom and Pop' store in the neighborhood and we, the wives, would run it. We got a good response from the neighbors. I stayed very busy.

My co-worker was lazy. She would come to work late or not at all. When she did work, she only wanted to sit behind the cash register. Yet she wanted half of the profits. I felt used and looked for a way to get out of the business. I asked my landlord if she would like to take on the store since she lived on the premises. She jumped at the chance and bought us out.

I now had too much time on my hands. Maybe I should have kept working at the store.

For the first year of our marriage, I dreaded going to bed. "Oh God, here goes this mess again." I tried to stay up until Al went to sleep and ease into bed beside him. One night something happened. I did not understand it. Whatever it was, I never wanted it to end. I wondered if I had fainted. After that night, I would wait for Al to come to bed. I finally got the hang of this sex thing.

A little while later, I got pregnant and I was all right

with that. My sister Maxine came to help me with the baby. We did not have insurance but we qualified for the Teen Pregnancy Clinic to deliver the baby.

An elderly black woman that assisted the black pregnant teenagers ran the clinic. The doctor was an old, mean, wrinkled white man. He reminded me of The Grinch Who Stole Christmas.

Al and Maxine took me to the clinic when my labor pains were about twenty minutes apart. They called the doctor. He came in looking like he forgot to comb his hair and that my problem had disturbed his much-needed rest.

I felt excruciating pain. Something was wrong. The baby would not come out. He had grown too big and I could not deliver him. I needed surgery and the clinic didn't have the special equipment on the premises.

The doctor told me to push a few times. He seemed to get impatient and forced his hand inside me to pull the baby out. He gave the baby to the nurse and left the room. I never saw him again. The nurse took the baby. I could only see the side of his face. He was such a big baby.

I went to sleep and woke expecting my baby beside me. I asked Maxine, "Where's my baby?"

"I'll go check," she said, leaving the room.

Al came in and I asked him, "Where is the baby? Why haven't I seen him yet?"

"That might be him crying now."

A whole day passed and I had not seen or held my baby yet. I was really getting pissed. Al, my sister and the nurse came into my room with gloomy looks on their faces

The nurse was the first to speak. "We have something to tell you. Please don't get upset. Your baby did not make it. The doctor said he was too large for you to deliver.

69

He weighed ten pounds. We did not want to tell you yet, fearing the news would make you hemorrhage."

"Al, what happened to the baby? I want to see him." "The doctor and I took care of it. Don't make a fuss now." That was all Al had to say.

I tried to find out what happened to my baby. I never received a birth certificate or death certificate--it was as though he had never been born. No one would answer my questions. I will always believe that the Doctor broke my baby's neck trying to deliver him and that's why they would not let me see him.

I grieved for my child for a long time. I had a vision of what he looked like since I only saw the side of his face. I gave him the name Osmond Orlando and wrote it the Family Bible along with a little history. In my mind and heart, he will forever be my angel in Heaven.

After a year, I got pregnant again. This time we had insurance and I had my baby in a hospital. I delivered Jerry, a big nine pound boy. Oh, how I loved this baby! He filled a void in my heart that I didn't know existed.

A year later, I got pregnant again. Oh, God. I did not expect this so soon. Jerry needs me, how will I have enough room in my heart to love both babies? I pictured myself playing with Jerry and forgetting the new baby. Please God, help me to have the ability to love them both.

Al's job came to a close. The government did not fund the Veterans school again so it closed. We needed to relocate again so Alvin could find a new job. Before Al could ask his parents if we could move in with them, Mama asked me to come home and have the baby, giving Al a chance to find employment.

I missed Mama so much. Being home with my best

friend in the world put a big smile on my face.

Al's mother did not like me very much and I did not have a lot of love for her. We were both tiny people. She weighed about ninety-eight pounds and I weighed one hundred four pounds. She said, "I can't understand why Al wanted that little thing." He was only five feet five himself. What could he do with a big woman?

When the baby was born, she came and asked me, "Who are you going to lay this child on? He is not my sons child because he cannot have children."

"What? He is your son. Why would you say that?" I asked.

"Because he is circumcised, that's why."

I tried to compose myself and be respectful to my elders, like Mama taught me. I shouted, "They didn't cut off his penis, just the skin around the head of it."

She looked stunned because I had never responded in that manner, no matter how she insulted me.

We moved in with Mama and Daddy. I was so thankful we would not have to travel on the highway from Jackson again. I feared we would be robbed again.

I thought about that cold, dark December night. It was about nine thirty and we traveled slowly in a beat up brown Hudson. It could not go any faster. We wanted to get home before Christmas. We were happy because we had saved one hundred and fifty dollars to buy Christmas gifts and help with other expenses. We heard a siren behind us and saw flashing lights. It was a highway patrolman signaling Al to pull over.

The officer walked to our car, shined his flashlight directly into Al's face and asked to see his driver's license.

71

"Why are you speeding, boy?

"I wasn't speeding."

"You callin' me a liar? Are you callin' me a liar? I said you was speeding; now let me see your driver's license." He shined the light in my face and asked, "Who's the little gal you got there?"

"She's my wife," Al answered.

Al tried to get his license out of his wallet when the officer snatched the wallet out of his hand and searched through it. He counted the money and put it back in the wallet. "Well boy, seems like you got yourself in a little trouble. You're going to have to see the judge and let him settle this. His office is up there a little ways. Follow me and don't try to get away."

We followed him a few miles down the dark road. He pulled into what looked like a raunchy roadhouse. At least four patrol cars were parked in the lot with the other cars. The music was loud. A big party must have been going on.

The officer came to Al. "Sit tight while I go get the judge. I wouldn't try to get away if I was you."

A different policeman came out to our car. He was eating candy from a See's candy box and said, "Boy, you must be the one doing all that speeding."

I think Al was just as scared as I was. I heard my heart thumping far too fast. Al did not answer his question.

He leaned close to Al smelling like alcohol and said, "I am the judge. Boy, you got two choices. Pay the fine of one hundred fifty dollars or go to jail. It's up to you."

All I could think was, Oh my God. I don't know where I am, I can't drive this car. If they take him to jail, what are they going to do to me out here in the middle of nowhere? I was scared speechless.

Al chose to pay the fine.

The officer did not give us a ticket or a receipt. He took the money and handed Al a partially eaten box of candy and said, "Merry Christmas boy, and stop all that speeding."

Al handed me the box of candy and I couldn't wait to roll down the window and toss the candy out on the highway. We were concerned about having enough gasoline to make it to our parents' home.

We celebrated Christmas as usual, but it was not the jolly good time.

After the holidays, Al found a job in the city doing alterations in a dry cleaning business. It didn't pay very well.

Al knew that Mama had not forgiven him for interrupting my life. He always tried to win her over. He would make a point to bring up the Bible when he was in her presence. She was a Christian and she began to think of him as a Christian also. I did not like the way Al tried to con her. He worked in the city but did not contribute to the household. I did not have a job and could not contribute anything but my service.

I was so concerned about Mama. She did not look good. She was only fifty-two years old, had lost her spunk, and had headaches too often. She was always worried about Daddy.

I came home to have the baby, which was due in February. Mama's health declined at an alarming rate. Daddy didn't give her much attention. She was lonely and felt neglected and sensed that Al and I were having the same problems.

I began having labor pains. Al had already sent

somebody to go and get his Aunt, the midwife, just in case I delivered while he was at work.

I did a little cleaning in my room between labor pains and a letter fell out of Al's jacket. He wrote the letter to the woman he had been chasing. I opened it and read what he tried to get over to her. She stood him up the weekend before. He stayed out all night, the night I had the baby.

The midwife looked like a jet-black clown, dressed up all in white. She smelled like Lysol. Her thick beard must have been the envy of most men. She was not a day under eighty years old. She entered the room with so much pride and confidence. Her total number of deliveries was in the hundreds. This delivery should be in the Guinness Book of Records.

She opened her authentic medical bag and removed the white rags made of torn sheets and placed them on two chairs. Her meds were several unlabeled bottles that she replaced into her bag. She finished her setup, climbed in the bed behind me with all of her clothes on, and started snoring like a grizzly bear. I was crying like a baby.

She woke up later, and asked, "Have you had the baby yet?"

"No. I'm in a lot of pain," I said.

She crawled over me, went to her bag and gave me a spoonful of liquid that looked like red cough syrup. T will always believe it was cough syrup. The pain increased and I cried out very loud. The baby was coming. I tried not to cry. I felt ashamed that everyone in the house could hear me having my baby. It was as if I was having a baby in front of the whole world.

I gave birth to a plump, healthy baby. I named him Waldo and I did have lots of love for him. I had enough for both my children. The realization felt wonderful.

Al came home on Saturday morning. I still suffered from after pains and was infuriated with him. He should have been there at all cost.

He looked at the baby and came to sit on the bed next to me. "He sure is cute," he said.

He had no idea that I had found the letter that he forgot to mail to her. His letter said he had waited all night for her the week before. He had told me the car broke down. The letter said, 'after all I did for you, you treat me like this?'

I made a hand written copy of the letter and hid the original. I then got his straight razor from his shaving kit and hid it under my pillow. This was my equalizer just in case he said I was lying to him.

He started making his excuses about why he hadn't come home. When I heard enough of his lies, I sat up, pulled the razor out from under the pillow and said, "Get your ass off this bed right now. I know her name, her address and what she means to you. I am going to write her and tell her to please take your sorry ass off my hands. Now get your ass out of this house and don't come back."

He left the room and sat in the car for hours. He might have been sleeping. He pleaded with me to let him back in the house. I let him back in but gave him the silent treatment. I did not want Mama to know what was going on.

Marriage for Sessy

Can two walk together, except they be agreed?

Amos 3:3

Chapter 7
Saying Goodbye to Mama

Mama's illness advanced at an alarming rate. Her sisters from Louisiana came and took her to a hospital in New Orleans, seeking a better treatment. She had been diagnosed with a rare form of liver cancer called Primary Sclerosis Collagist.

I always thought drinking too much alcohol caused liver cancer. Mama did not drink and she did not allow Daddy to bring his alcohol in the house. "Not over my children," she would say. Mama never even tasted his drinks, yet she was the one with liver disease.

Mama's condition did not improve. I could see her slipping away. She could not assist me with the birth of my son as she had planned.

The neighbors came and gave us a hand whenever they could. Mama was well loved by the neighbors. Her beautiful flourishing garden had helped to feed so many of them.

Mama's mother was half Choctaw Indian and Black. Mama learned so much from her. I believe her gardening skills came from her mother. She grew vegetables that no one in the community had ever heard of. She grew a vegetable called 'Rapes'. This green vegetable is now used to make canola oil. Her eggplants surprised everyone. Only a few knew how to cook it.

She got the Red Indian Peach seed from her parents. Mama made a mixture of peach tree leaves steeped in water and shampooed our hair to keep it soft and thick. We all had thick heads of hair.

She planted sassafras trees. We used the bark to make root beer and make a hot tea that tasted so good and healed whatever ailed you.

She lost interest in all the things that made her happy. I felt helpless and wanted to comfort her. However, I went into labor and gave birth to an eight and a half pound boy.

The neighbors continued to assist both of us. Their daily visits meant so much to me. Especially since mama insisted that, I act like an invalid. I felt like the birth giving part was the main event and now I should just get up and go. When Mama had her babies, her mother made her stay inside for a whole month. She kept the curtains closed to protect the baby's eyes. No hair shampoos or lifting heavy items. I was not allowed to cook or clean house. Thank God, for the neighbors who cooked and sat by her bed and consoled her during her painful episodes.

As soon as my after pains from giving birth subsided, I resumed my role as nurse, housekeeper, mother and good listener to Mama. She worried mostly about leaving her two youngest children, eleven-year-old Dean and thirteen-year-old Lynn. I was not prepared to lose Mama yet. She was the biggest part of my life.

I was trying to take care of a newborn and Mama. Mama's sister had been taking care of the baby. I named him Waldo but she had nicknamed him Mickey. She really got attached to him. When he turned six weeks old, she begged me to let her raise him. She had had eight miscarriages and really wanted a child. Of course, I said no, "I have to raise him myself."

Mama needed round the clock care now. Our family doctor would drop by to check on her whenever he could. We had very little money to pay for his visits. She had no insurance.

I tried so hard to help her get better. Whenever I gave her a bath she expressed shame saying, "I never thought my child would see my nakedness."

"But Mama, you bathed me when I could not. Now it's my turn to bathe you."

She was in constant unbearable pain. All I could do was hold her hand and place a cold towel on her head. There were times when she could not eat. I would freeze juice, crush it and put it in her mouth. At one point, she went blind for a whole week. I felt so helpless. I would have done anything to ease her pain.

"Sessy, I feel like I am in labor all the time," she said.

It became evident that she needed to be hospitalized. All her family lived in Louisiana. We had to use their address to get her into a hospital there. The one in Mississippi was a hundred miles away and they would not always accept blacks unless they had good insurance.

My sister and I took turns staying with her at the hospital. We took shifts around the clock to make sure she was never alone.

There were days I prayed for God to take her out of pain. I knew she would not get well at this point.

On August 7, 1953, the angel of death came for Mama and gave her eternal peace.

The days that followed were hectic, making plans for the funeral, whom to involve in the ceremony, getting her sons home from the military and just keeping our wits about us. In my mind, she was not dead. She was just somewhere else and would be back soon.

I looked back on the things she did to prepare me for her death. She took me to the bank and had me sign on her account so I could handle her affairs when she was unable to. She asked me to look after my brother and sister. She encouraged me to continue to believe in God and stay the kind of person I am.

She told me, "Of all the children I have, you are the only one who never talked back to me. I gave you lots of whippings but not one was for talking back. You always kept your promise. "

I remembered her stroking me on the cheek with the back of her hand when she was pleased with me. I was not ready for this final episode. I still expected her to call for me and the desire was so real I would rush to her, sure she had called. However, she had left the house weeks before to go to the hospital.

I don't remember much about her funeral. It's a big blob in my mind. Too many well-wishers voiced their thoughts about her and some barely knew her. There was a lot of crying and shouting. I lost control when the casket closed for the final time. It was very traumatic for me.

The following days were not much better. We got rid of all the medical equipment and gave some of her clothes to a cousin who wore the same size.

We all felt that Daddy held some of the blame for her death. After all, he had not been a loving husband to her. One of my sisters decided to play a prank on Daddy and make him look the fool. We all went along with it.

As soon as he was nearby, one of us shouted, "Look!

Look at all this money. Where do you think she got all this money?"

Daddy didn't budge an inch. He knew we were lying.

Family members returned to their homes and that's when the isolation and pain of losing Mama set in. Mama was gone and I would never see her again.

Dean went to live with our brother Larry, who lived in Bogalusa, Louisiana. He needed to be closer to a school because the school near us had closed.

That day while I was sitting on the porch everything went black. "I can't see! I can't see!"

I slapped my face, shook my head, bucked my eyes, still the darkness remained. After a moment, my sight returned. I went to bed and slept for ten hours.

A few weeks later, my aunt decided to take my sister Lynn home with her. She didn't think it right that Al drove her to school but that was the only transportation she had. I hated to see her leave, but I agreed with her knowing Al's reputation.

Soon after, I discovered I was pregnant. This time, I insisted on getting a real doctor because we had insurance. He was a black doctor that made house calls. In my ninth month, I gave birth to a handsome boy. We named him Tony Ray. My three boys were my life. We had so much fun together, I felt like a kid again.

Al and I continued to live with Daddy. Dad and I got along well. Everyone said I was his pet anyway. He did not care much for Al, but he tolerated him. Al had a bad rep for chasing girls. He would know because he was a chaser himself. Our stay came to a sharp end the day Daddy heard Al talking about him behind his back.

Al did not know that Daddy was home sitting in the

house by an open window. Al was outside talking to a neighbor. "You know that old man is crazy. He doesn't have much sense."

Daddy bolted out of the house. "I heard what you said! You little ol' peanut head bastard, get your ass off my property...now or I will go get that '38 special and blow your damn head off."

The neighbor tried to quiet Daddy down while Al jumped into the car and sped off leaving the kids and me. If he had returned before Daddy cooled down, I do believe Daddy would have blown his head off.

Al waited a few days and came back to pick us up. He found an old run-down house somebody had abandoned. They had moved to Chicago. He had located the owners and they agreed to let us live there rent-free if Al would fix it up to livable condition.

When I saw the house, I almost fainted. "You mean we are supposed to live in that haunted looking house?"

"Oh, we can fix it up," he said.

The living room had a wood heater and nothing else. The bedroom had a broken down dresser, a bed frame and a wood chair. The kitchen had an apartment size stove, a small table and a tub sink with an old type faucet that hooked up to the water hose outside. The steps had fallen down by the back door and a box sat in their place. The storage shed looked better than the house.

We had to stay with his parents while he worked on the house. His parents lived about two miles back in the woods on eighty acres of land they had bought for sixteen hundred dollars. His father raised a variety of vegetables for the canning plants downtown. He had a wagon and two very big mules. He would fill it with melons, fruit, vegetables and sugar cane. He drove it right down Main Street along with the cars. Nobody ever tried to stop him. I wondered, simple-mindedly if it was because he was a tall, muscular, very black Jamaican, with a thick accent. He would park his wagon on a side street and sell everything he had.

He grew to be my best friend in the whole world. I would sneak food to him when Al's mother thought he had enough. He would give me money when he thought I was broke.

Al got in a fight with his mother, which was not unusual. He defended his father from her often. However, this time he decided to leave and move into the ghost looking house before it was finished.

I felt like a hobo living like that. I tried to keep my family away so they could not see the horrible condition. Al had not fixed the house and it smelled like old canvas dipped in dirty oil. He had nailed canvas over the windows to keep the cold out. He used his tailoring skills to sew together strips of the smelly dirty canvas and create a partition between the living room and the kitchen. There was no bathroom inside and we had to use an outhouse. It had to be the only one left in the city.

I made friends with a few of the neighbors. I did not want to be seen coming out of that house. Mama would turn over in her grave if she knew how I was living.

My old home economics teacher lived a few doors down from us. I tried to hide from her because I did not want her to see the house in that condition. I tried to fix the inside to look livable. Al told her I was home and sent her to visit me so I could not hide that day. She saw the chenille bedspread that I made, admired it and asked me to teach her how to make one. We would sit on my porch for hours working on that bedspread.

I had too much idle time on my hands. I found a few customers who would let me do their hair so I could make a few dollars. I located the owner of the empty lot next door and asked him if I could plant a garden there. He said yes. Al's father was happy to help me. He came, plowed the whole lot, and gave me a variety of seeds, corn, peas, carrots, okra and string beans. It was enough for us to feed the whole neighborhood. The kids and I worked and had fun in that garden.

They loved to pick up bugs and put them in a jar. One day, I heard Waldo scream ouch. I rushed to him and found Jerry hitting him in the head with a baseball bat.

"He won't stand still. I am trying to kill those bees that's on his head," Jerry said.

I grabbed the bat from Jerry and rushed Waldo into the house to treat him. I could not tell which knots the bees or the bat made. I treated them all with a paste made with baking soda and water. The swelling went away soon after. This was one of Mama's medical remedies she had passed on to me.

Al had started an affair with a woman nearby. He did not try to be subtle about it. It was the talk of the neighborhood. The albino looking woman was so proud of her catch. She did not get any fight out of me. I had lost all respect and what little love I had for him long before she came into the picture. I wanted to leave him, but I felt stuck. I was stuck, and embarrassed by his treatment.

I made friends with and elderly neighbor that lived across the street from me. She would go walking with the boys and me when she felt like it. One day, she was visiting us and asked, "What are you cooking for dinner?"

I could not tell her that I had nothing to cook. Somehow, she felt that I did not.

She said, "I have a blackberry bush on my back fence. Come, let's pick some and you can make a blackberry dumpling pie." She gave me the flour for the pie, stayed, and ate dinner with us. I was so grateful and ashamed.

I knew that I needed to make a change and soon all I could think about was getting away. Where would I go? I had three kids, no job and no money.

In the back of my mind, I heard my mother's words, "Sessy you stay with Al he is the kid's father. All kids need both parents. Just stay through thick and thin."

I never learned the difference between the two, they were both so bad. I never stopped thinking about making a better life for my boys and myself.

Maxine, my oldest sister, had moved to California a few years before. I thought about moving to be near her, but the kids were so young, two, four and six. How would we get there? Where would the money come from? How much money would I need? It would take three days by bus. Could the kids make that trip and survive?

I prayed to God every day. "Please help us get out of this dreadful house."

One hot day in July 1956, God answered my prayer. Al told me that one of his friends heard about the good job opportunities opening up in Alameda, California. "I was thinking about moving out there. Do you think you could ask your sister Maxine if we could stay with her until we get our own place?"

"Yes, oh yes," I said. "I'll go to the phone booth and call her tomorrow."

The morning did not come fast enough. Maxine was

glad to know that we were planning to come. She said she would clear it with her husband and let me know.

I hated to leave my beautiful garden. It was in full bloom and the corn and black-eyed peas were ready for picking. I told all my neighbors of our plans to leave and I would like them not to let my garden go to waste. "Please eat from the garden and tell your friends also. Take turns watering it and it will last the rest of the summer.

We spent the next few days dismantling the house and giving away the few good things of use. The kids and I moved in with Al's parents. He connected with his friends and took off for California. We would join him as soon as he secured a job.

The months that we stayed in his mother's home were pure hell. She treated me like a slave. If the kids and I decided to hike in the woods, she would lock us out if we were gone too long. The refrigerator was off limits without her permission. I endured it because it was not going to be forever.

Al found a job but not a place to stay. Maxine said we could stay with her while we looked for a place of our own.

Al had negotiated with a woman that would be driving to California to bring our three kids and me for a fee. She over loaded her car. When she came to pick us up, she already had five people in the car. I had to squeeze into the back middle seat and hold one child in my lap; one on the floor between my legs and the other one shared my seat. It was so hot the kids got fevers and my butt got blisters form sitting on the clear plastic seat covers.

The drivers got tired on the second day and started drinking too much. I had never learned to drive and I didn't drink. They kept getting lost. I would tell them, "You are on the wrong highway."

"How do you know? Coming out of them woods, you've not been anywhere."

"What do you know? You've probably never been out of those woods," I said. "We are supposed to be on highway ten and we're on highway forty seven."

They stopped at a service station to get directions back to the right highway. I could read a map very well and on the third day, they allowed me to navigate. We never got lost again. When we neared our destination, I saw a shortcut on the map and we arrived in Alameda before dark.

We all looked and smelled like a hot mess, but I knew this move was right for me and I would find a way to have a better life for my boys and myself.

Saying Goodbye to Mama

To proclaim the acceptable year of the Lord, and the
day of vengeance of our God; to comfort all that mourn;

Isaiah 61:2

Chapter 8
Home in California

After three full days of traveling, our car finally pulled up in front of my sister's house. Even though she lived in the housing project, it looked like a mansion to me. My kids had a temperature and I had trouble sitting down. Maxine and I embraced in a joyful manner. We had truly missed each other.

My first task was to clean up the children and get them into fresh clothes. Maxine helped me to get dressed. She saw the blisters on my butt and covered them with Vaseline. She had cooked us a good, hot meal of fried chicken with all the trimmings. The kids were glad to see their cousins again. Al had a part time job at the post office. When he got home, we embraced. He turned and picked up our two-year-old son Tony. Al was amazed at his being able to walk.

Tony said, "Hi Daddy."

"Wow he can talk now! Gee he was a baby when I left."

Our living arrangement went well. We paid half the rent and bought half the food. I did most of the cooking. Maxine said I was better at it than she was. I worked hard so that I would not be a burden to my sister. Her house consisted of a living room, dining room, kitchen, three bedrooms and one bathroom. This space accommodated ten people quite well.

Maxine's personality was quite different from mine. She did not hesitate to say what she meant and mean what she said. Maxine told her husband off any time he would say something crazy. Al hated that, and he made remarks about her disrespect toward her husband.

One night they got into a fight about the woman next door. Maxine heard that her husband was having an affair with the woman and said, "I don't see what you would want with that ugly woman any way."

He laughed and said "It not the beauty it's the booty."

She was ironing clothes at the time. She yelled, "You son of a bitch." and threw the hot iron at him barely missing his head. He jumped up laughed again ran into the other room and closed the door.

Al got so mad at her he paced the floor. It wasn't my fight and I didn't want to get in the middle of them, so I went to our room, sat on the bed and started reading the newspaper.

He followed me and stopped in the doorway. "Go check on the kids and see if they are covered up."

He was closer to them. All he needed to do was turn around and he could see if they were covered or not.

I said okay and kept reading, planning to go when I finished that sentence. I was looking down at the newspaper when Al balled up his fist hit me smack in my mouth, breaking the tip off my bottom front tooth. I was shocked he had never hit me before.

"Don't you start that with me trying to act like your sister. I said get up and go check on the kids."

I touched my lip and it was bleeding, when I saw that blood on my hand I think I turned into a real lion. I let out a growl, bit my lip and curled my fingers toward his face, clawing his entire face from his forehead to his chin.

My scratches made his face look like he was looking through a fence. He wore that face for weeks. He didn't know I could have used makeup to conceal the scars. However, I felt he needed to see that fence every time he looked in the mirror.

After I scratched him, he knocked me down and stomped on me until my brother-in-law stopped him. I became hysterical and could not stop crying.

Maxine felt that a ride in the car would cool thing down. I told Maxine my plans. I wanted to get a job as soon as possible anywhere I could. She told me that her friend worked at the cannery at night and she would ask her to help get me a job and I could ride with her. I was already fixing hair in the kitchen and saving at least half of that income. I was hired on the same night shift and could ride with her.

I had never made that much money before. After I had accumulated five checks, I secretly opened a bank account. I told Maxine in secret about my savings. I thought someone should know in case something happened to me. She broke her promise and told her husband.

One Saturday a salesman came by selling cookware. Maxine's husband asked to borrow a hundred dollars from me. "I sure would like to get those pots for the wife. Since so many people lives here we need more pots."

"I don't have that much money on me. I could let you have it the next week."

He did not believe me. I had put it in a savings account and could not get it out on the weekend. I even showed him a check that I was planning to cash. He got angry, went behind my back, and told Al about the money that I was

91

saving.

Thank God, I never told Maxine how much I had saved. Al tried every way he could to find out if I had money saved. I never did admit that I had any money. But I continued to save every other check.

I knew it was time to move out of their house. My sister Lynn had moved to Los Angeles, nearly 500 miles away. I made plans to take my three boys and move near her. My bank account was getting pretty big. I asked Lynn to look for an apartment near her.

She was looking for me, when an unexpected thing happened. I got pregnant again. I had worked so hard to prevent getting pregnant--my baby was four years old for goodness sake. I could not take three kids to my sisters and be pregnant. I had to change my plans. This meant waiting another year or two to move. I really hated living in the projects especially for the kid's sake.

I figured if I had to stay on with Al, that I could at least leave the project. I got a real estate agent to look for a small house in a good neighborhood. He located one in my price range with a huge back yard perfect for the boys and a garden for me. I paid the down payment with the money I had saved to relocate to Los Angeles. Al never knew about the money. I made all of the transactions. He just bragged about being a homeowner.

Oh how I loved being a homeowner. Daddy always told us to try hard to own our own home. He impressed all eight of us to try to be fortunate enough to be homeowners. We fulfilled his wish.

I had obtained my beautician license from Mississippi but I needed to get a California license. I met a woman in the grocery store, who was attending the same beauty school that I wanted to attend. She offered me a ride if I could get to her house on time every morning. I was in a hurry to get started before my stomach got too big.

I completed my test before the State Board of Cosmetology in my eighth month of pregnancy. One of the applicants congratulated me for being so brave to take the test so late in my pregnancy. She laughed and said,"Girl you didn't have to pass the test they just gave it to you to get you out of here before you had that baby." I laughed with her and thanked God for my California Cosmetology License.

The baby arrived a few weeks later, it was our first girl, and I was so delighted to have a daughter. We named her Pamela. She was my pride and joy. I tried to teach her many things. She was my little helper. She would get teased about her little fat cheeks; it did not seem to bother her one bit. Her brothers called her bossy. Al was also glad to have a girl in the family. By this time, I had built up a clientele doing hair in the kitchen. I needed more space in the house. A friend of ours owned a demolition business in San Francisco, just across the Bay Bridge. He told us how much good material he threw away every day. We asked him to let us have some it to add rooms on the back of our house. He was happy to set aside any lumber he thought we could use. This saved him from paying larger dump fees.

Al got his brothers to help him collect this lumber and put it in our back yard. My job was to pull out all the old nails from the lumber and stack it by length in neat piles. One of the nosey neighbors called the fire department and reported us for creating a fire hazard. The Fireman came and found me out in the back yard pulling nails out of a two-by-four. I told him our plans. He informed me of who had called, and said she called them often, complaining on everyone. They have to come out and check. He told me to continue to do what I was doing and wished me good luck on our project.

We added four rooms and two baths with that free lumber--two rooms and a bath up stairs and two rooms and a bath down stairs. One of the rooms would be my beauty shop. I learned to install hardwood floors, paint and texture walls, put up sheetrock, pick up parts for the electrician and plumber and any other materials that were needed.

It took all of two years to finish, and it was worth all the blood sweat and tears I experienced. I had learned new skills and wanted to make use of what I had learned during the building process. I had mastered the use of a skill saw. I installed hardwood floors using a nail gun. I sanded the floor evenly and stained it to a shiny finish.

I asked Al to think about buying old houses and fix them up with all the free material we were getting. We could rent or sell them at a good profit. He wanted no part of investing in anything. He said I should be grateful for what God had given me already.

Our second daughter was born, making a total of five children. We named her Jeanine, she was long and lanky with a very light complexion, and her facial features were the same as Al's mother.

I had almost miscarried while I was pregnant with Jeanine. While I was in my first trimester of pregnancy Al got angry with me because I went to a Stanly cookware party with his brother and wife and had not asked him first. He nagged all night. It was a Sunday morning. The lack of sleep had taken its toll on me.

While I was cooking a breakfast of bacon and eggs,

94

coffee and toast Al came into the kitchen to give me his final threat. "If you ever leave this house without my knowing I will put you out. Do you hear me?"

I rose up like a mad tiger and shouted back at him. "I am not going anywhere. If anybody leaves, it will be your stupid ass. I paid the whole down payment on this house while you were out screwing other women."

Al hit me upside my head. I stumbled back picked up the pan of bacon off the stove, slung the whole pan at Al, hitting his bare shoulders. He was furious, and knocked me down and put his knee on my stomach and was slapping my face when his brother heard my screams and came to my rescue.

His brother said, "Man what's wrong with you? She waited for you to come home. You did not, so we took her on with us and brought her back. Man you are a fool."

I was sore for days. I couldn't even hang the clothes on the line. Black blood secreted from my vagina for three days. I had no idea that I was pregnant with Jeanine.

My life with Al was getting worse. I swore to God this would be my last child. I concocted some medical reason and said the doctor had advised me to avoid having more children and that we should always use condoms. He did not want me to purchase the condoms because it was not 'lady like.' Al found a place that sold them by the case. I felt that I was safe.

Not two years later Ellen was born. I will always believe Al damaged the condoms. Ellen was a hefty, plump, dark skinned baby. She was the spitting image of Al's sister. I loved his sister, we always got along well. Everybody spoiled Ellen because she was such a spunky child who started cursing before she could make a complete sentence.

95

However, she did have the good sense to not let me hear her say 'bad' words. I just happened to run upon her cursing her brothers out.

They found it funny when she came into their room wearing only a diaper and yelled, "Alright you mother fuckers get your ass out of bed right now, and go to school."

I was shocked. Where did she get that from? We never spoke such language. It was the baby sitters husband. All his conversations were laced with profanity. He might say, 'Good morning, God damn-it.' I knew that I needed to find another babysitter.

I never learned how to drive a car. It was easier and cheaper for Al to take the bus to work. For fifty cents each way, he walked one block to the bus stop, and it put him off in front of his work place. We had a car, so I decided I would learn to drive. I would ask everybody to help me. Someone taught me to park. Another took me around the block. I sought out any kind of help to figure out this driving business. Al did not know of my accomplishment because the kids and I had not told him.

It was so nice to drive to the schools, get grocery and do the other things I needed to do. The kids helped me with my driving by telling when it was safe to change lanes. They watched the gas gauge and reminded me when it was time to stop by 'Dollar Ethyl' to get gas. I would always give the attendant a dollar and say, "Ethyl please."

I got bold one rainy day and decided to pick Al up from work. The kids were so proud of me.

Al was pissed about it. "You don't have any license. Move over let me drive."

The kids started screaming, "No Daddy she drove down here let her drive back she can drive."

The next day Al decided to drive instead of taking the bus. I forgot he was a fool. I really did not think he would take the car from us.

We were back on the bus again. We did not miss our annual back to school dinner we looked forward to every year. All six of my kids would follow me on the bus to the same diner. It was called Mel's Diner. We would put on our best clothes as though we were going to church.

Jerry would take care of Jeanine and I carried Ellen in my arms. Waldo and Tony would watch Pamela. The cost friendly menu let the kids order anything they wanted. Waldo decided that he wanted to be a vegetarian. His brother's laughed at him because he never stopped eating meat, and lots of it.

He ordered a stack of pancakes with a side of bacon. After he almost finished his bacon he asked me, "Mother is there any meat in this bacon?"

"Not one bit son. Not one bit." We took the bus home. Tomorrow we would shop for school clothes.

Now that he drove the car, Al gave a ride to a woman from his job. I had to get up an hour earlier to get his breakfast and allow time to pick her up. She smoked and Al didn't. All the cigarettes butts had lipstick on them and were in his ashtray. She sat closer to his tray than hers.

"Al, would you take Jerry to school today? He has a swollen jaw and I don't want him getting soaked in the rain."

"I don't have time. I'll be late," he said.

I was so mad. He had time to pick up that woman before work but couldn't drive his own son to school. I worried and waited for Jerry to come home to see if he was alright.

That very day, we bundled up and walked three miles

to a used car lot. I found an old light blue Chevrolet. The dealer let me have it for three hundred dollars. I gave him fifty dollars down and made payments for the balance. He gave me the keys and I drove it home.

The kids stayed near me when it was time for Al to come home. They knew he would be real pissed.

"Whose car is that in the driveway?"

"Mine."

He picked up an end table to throw at me. Jerry grabbed Al's hand and clenching his teeth he said, "Don't you hit her."

"Who does she think she is? Going out and buying a car. I am the head of this house. It's just a pile of junk anyway."

I kept that little car until Tony and his friends wrecked it on the freeway. Tony hit a big truck and the truck flipped over on its side. Thank God, no one was hurt and the police were not called. The truck owner told Tony that he could leave. He felt God had spared him and he had insurance. The tow truck flipped the truck back over and everything worked out fine.

With the Beauty shop complete, I made several trips to city hall to get the proper papers. It took quite a while, but opening day was a joy. I could watch the kids and work. The den was next to the shop. I monitored their schoolwork and the exact time they made it home. They had to report to me the minute they arrived and change clothes before eating their snacks.

Two of Al's brothers, who left the military, returned to Mississippi but could not find jobs. Al invited them to come and live with us. He only charged them a whopping five dollars a week and I had to fix their lunches out of that.

I did not complain about them because my teenage brother lived with us and attended the local high school. Being so young, he could not contribute anything.

The beauty shop grew and Al resented my success. He would eavesdrop at the den door. He could not figure out why we laughed so much. He continued to drink too much. Oh, he never missed church, no matter how drunk he was.

One day Al eavesdropped at the beauty shop door. The kids called the shop phone. "Daddy is listening at the shop door."

I tiptoed to the door, got a good grip, and pushed it open with all my might, giving him a bump on his forehead.

"What are you doing? I didn't know you were standing there," I said, all innocence and smiles. He got pretty angry. There were far too many ladies in the shop for him to react like he wanted too.

Jerry and Waldo liked music. They always played the latest records, singing along. I looked for something I could afford to assist them in learning more about music. I had tried to learn to play the piano, but found myself too busy to continue the lessons. I found a music store and rented a used piano for ten dollars a month.

Jerry had a friend who took music lessons nearby. I signed Jerry and Waldo up for weekly piano lessons. Waldo studied the flute in school and became a good flutist. In fact, his teacher used him to demonstrate the flute at other schools.

After a few years of lessons, Jerry organized a band and named it the Afro Blue Ensemble. They played at small parties for tips. He landed a big gig at the University of California Berkeley. Someone from KTVU Channel 2 television station in Oakland attended and invited them to the station to play background music.

Waldo studied to become an actor. He played the leading role in his high school play, Man on the Moon. The first night of the play Waldo came down with a high temperature. I called the school informing them that he would not be there because of his illness. The principle begged me to please allow him to come. He offered to come pick him up, let him perform, and bring him right back.

Waldo wanted to be there. He was the leading man. "Please let me go?"

"Only if they take me to...in case you get worse and have to go to the hospital."

I did not recognize my son. His performance was excellent. An agent watched in the audience. He was scouting for actors for a movie that would be filmed in Oakland in a few weeks, The Mack. The agent told Waldo's teacher he would like Waldo to be sure and come to the upcoming audition.

The beauty shop grew very fast. I hired three more operators and that little shop was packed as tight as a can of sardines. I had worked as a stylist in a weave shop before I opened my own. I could not weave and she could not style hair. She sent her clients to me to get styled after she completed their weaves. The clients complained about having to go to two different shops to get their hair done. One woman told me how much money she had left at the weave shop. She would be glad to give it to me.

I did not want to stab my friend in the back. After all, she sent me customers. I gave it some thought. I went to her and said, "I am being asked to weave. I will pay whatever you ask to teach me. Your sister-in law is coming out of beauty school soon. She could be your stylist."

"No way," she said. "I promised the lady that taught me to weave that I would not teach anyone else."

I went home feeling defeated. I was determined to add weaving to my services. I set Pamela in a recliner chair and proceeded to twist and turn the hair hoping it would hold the bangs that I had sewn into her hair. Pamela slept through all of it. She did not wake up until after midnight wearing bangs that I had removed from a dolls head.

I went back to my friend to ask her to sell me a piece of real hair and to tell her that I was teaching myself to weave.

"Oh Lord you are fixing to mess somebody up," she said. "Come on back and I will teach you how to weave, but you must promise me you will never teach anyone else."

I promised that I would not. I learned in two days and paid her what she asked of me. We have always remained friends. She had diabetes and her health took a turn for the worse. I rearranged my customer's around her schedule and went to her shop to service her customers until she recovered. She got worse and was unable to keep her shop open. I allowed her to bring her customer to my shop whenever she felt well enough to work. I felt I owed her so much. Her referrals increased my business greatly. My friend went into a diabetic coma and passed away. I will forever miss her.

Everything at our house changed faster than I had expected. One day I found there were no little kids down the hall for me to watch. After our third daughter arrived, I promised God I would not have any more children as long as they made birth control pills.

Al thought it a sin to take the pill. "God put us on earth

to replenish."

I said, "It is not. Them six kids is plenty."

The pills came packaged in a little round pack like no other pack. To keep down any problem between Al and me I emptied the little pink pills into a baby aspirin bottle and discarded the round container. One day he saw me take one he asked me what I was taking.

"Baby aspirin. Do you want one?" I would have given him one if he had said yes.

Where are all the kids? I miss them. The noise, the fights, the teasing--the den was empty now. They were all busy doing their own thing.

Jerry joined the army after the family tragedy. Tony was in his last year of high school. Pamela made head cheerleader at school. Ellen hated going to school and didn't do well. She played hooky often, and started gambling in study hall using her lunch money to make bets.

Jeanine paid too much attention to the boys, far too young. I tried to slow her down by letting her enroll in a modeling school that she had interest in attending. I got up early every Saturday and took her across the Bay Bridge to San Francisco. She attended The Barbizon School of Modeling.

I hoped this would give her some class and self-esteem. She started sneaking out of the house at night at age thirteen. I knew the danger she faced dating boys too old for her. She knew how to get between me and Al, causing conflict between us. It got to the point where I thought she needed counseling. The school offered free sessions and I enrolled the three of us. Al and Jeanine sat there and created a whole new household. Not one thing they said was true. Three sessions were all I could take.

102

My little shop busted at the seams. I needed to move, like, yesterday. On my day off, I started looking for a good location. Pamela and I were walking down a street in Berkeley looking at possible places and a good area for my beauty shop, not too far off the main streets. A for rent sign hung in the window of a building on this busy street. I walked next door to inquire about the empty space. He happened to be the owner and told me it was still available.

It was just what I wanted. It had been an auto repair shop. It was very filthy, and had old car parts from front to back. The owner told me the previous occupant paid one hundred sixty dollars a month but he was raising the rent to two hundred a month, "as is." He didn't know I would have paid him three hundred for this perfect location.

"Let us look around first." We walked out back of the building. An old couple lived back there.

Pamela said, "Oh Mother, don't get this ugly place it's a mess."

She could not see what I saw--a beautiful salon in a perfect location. A straight shot from the Bay Bridge, in front of the bay area rapid transit (BART) that would bring clients from San Francisco, Richmond, Walnut Creek, San Jose and the entire Bay area. It was close to downtown, had access to all freeways and was not too far from home.

I asked him to get the lease ready for me to sign the next day. When I arrived, I asked him to give me a lease for five years. He was shocked but very happy to do so. I had my mind set on a bigger place in the future but this ensured that he could not raise my rent for five years.

I employed several individuals to help me gut the place. The ceiling was cracked, the floor uneven, and the restroom did not have a wash bowl just a toilet. In the meantime, I looked for pretty equipment at a low cost. I found a place that sold used beauty shop items. They had perfect beautiful blue matching stations, chairs and dryers. The reception desk fit perfectly. We covered the floors in soft blue and black. I bought light colored cloth and made drapes by laying the cloth on the floor, and cutting it to fit the big picture window. A small private room sat in the back corner to shield the ladies that had little hair.

I went all out for the grand opening, which occurred two months after we really opened. My nephew (Maxine's son) owned a limo service and donated his services "to get you there auntie, in style. You must open with a bang."

I gladly accepted his offer.

He said, "Now, you can't be on time. Everybody must see when you arrive."

"Boy, you know I don't like being late. If you're not here by a certain time I am driving myself."

He came early because he knew I would leave without him. I looked up and saw a Bentley pulling up into my driveway. A tall man dressed in a black suit and cap got out and opened the door. I almost fell over. It was my nephew.

"Oh, hell no…a Bentley! Where in the hell did you get that?" I was looking for a regular old limo. I had never been inside of a Bentley. I felt embarrassed and did not want to ride in it. This was a show for the rich and I was far from being well off. He convinced me to ride to the opening.

When we arrived, the crowd was huge. I was not expecting such a big group; my shop could not accommodate that many people. He opened the door to the Bentley and chaperoned me out. The crowd roared and cheered. I smiled and waved but still felt embarrassed.

The months that followed were great. I hired more operators because the shop was always full. The Landlord saw all the activity and tried to raise the rent.

"No I have a lease for five years."

He complained about the water bill. "You need to help me pay it because of the increase of usage."

"I understand. Give me the water bill and I will pay all of it." The monthly bill was less than twenty dollars.

He tried to get me to pay the insurance on the building because he could be sued if I damaged someone's hair. I refused to pay because I had insurance on my business. He asked me on a date, but that was totally out of the question. The improvement that I made in the shop impressed him. On weekends, when I was closed, he would take his friends in the shop to see 'his beauty shop' that stayed busy all the time.

Pamela, my oldest daughter, helped on Saturdays doing non-stylist things like cleaning, working the desk, washing hairpieces and picking up food for the whole staff. She hated her job working on the military base. And realized she could make more money working with me.

I thought she should keep her job. I didn't want to be disappointed if she decided to leave me when I started to depend on her. She quit the job and came in full time with me.

The next three years were what I call, my most frugal years. I saved as much as I could. We ate beans and Raman noodles often. The fourth year, I checked out other salons to see what they were offering and what made them stand out from all the others. I would get a manicure at each salon to gather information. I attended many educational Seminars learning as much as I could about the beauty business.

I had saved enough money for a down payment on a building for my dream salon when tragedy hit again. This was a tragedy that changed the lives of the entire family.

Home in California

Again, the kingdom of heaven is like unto treasure hid in
a Field; the which when a man hath found, he hideth,
and for Joy therefore goeth and selleth all that he hath,
and buyeth that field.

Matthew 13:44

Chapter 9
Thirst for Education

No matter how many tragedies I had through the years, I have always hung onto Mama's words. "Sessy get an education. If you don't get anything else get an education," Mama said, "I did not get the chance to go to school like my brothers and sisters. I am the oldest child and my father said he needed my help in the fields. The fifth grade is all the education that I got. I want more for you. You are smart enough to be anything you want to be. I cannot help you learn much because I don't know much. You search to find the answers and I know you will make something of yourself."

Those words created a burning thirst for learning. I wanted to know everything. I would teach myself new things.

At age ten, I sharpened two sticks and taught myself to knit. I could only make strings and belts. Mama bought me a Teach Yourself Knitting book for ten cents. I was knitting right after that. I did not like knitting it was too slow. I tried crocheting and learned to make beanies and a few other things. I knitted booties, caps and sweaters for my babies, even made a pineapple tablecloth, which ended my knitting and crochet career.

Mama sent me to beauty school when I was in the ninth

grade. It felt so good to be the only beauty operator in the neighborhood. I took writing classes through the mail. I really wanted to become a writer. Rod Sterling, the Actor, had advertised one of the classes I took. I was gullible enough to think that he was really my instructor.

While Al was at work and the kids were at school I found free classes to attend. I took classes at Church, the library; anywhere they listed free classes in the newspaper.

After losing Waldo, I went back to school to get my Associate Degree in Child Development.

It was hard because Alvin felt like it was a waste of good time. He thought I should be doing something constructive.

A few months later, I enrolled at San Francisco State University. I obtained a Bachelor of Art degree in Home Economics with emphases on Nutrition.

Al threw fits about it. All the meals were ready when he got home, and the kids did their homework. I attended school three full days and worked in the beauty shop three days. I attended church most Sundays.

I soon realized the B.A. degree only pointed out just how little I knew about the universe. I enrolled in the Master's degree program at San Francisco State University and graduated with a Master's degree in nutrition.

Mama had been gone for many years, but her words echoed in my ears "Sessy you are so small in stature, get an education make something of yourself."

That is when I decided to go further in school. I found a Nutrition PhD program that I wanted to enroll in. It was a unique situation that I could handle. It was an eighteen-month program offering monthly payments for tuition. They held monthly classes at a nice hotel in South San

Francisco. All the instructors were Doctors, giving lectures on the four books that I received in the mail monthly. I studied the books and prepared to take the test on the last day of the monthly sessions.

These classes were held all over the United States. Headquarters was located in Southern California.

My graduation was held on the Queen Mary ship, built by Howard Hughes. The plane he built that never left the ground. I was so proud, just so proud of my accomplishments. I had studied so hard completing my dissertation--The Integumentary System, a Study of the Skin, Hair and Nails.

Daddy deserves some of the credit for encouraging us to work hard to be independent. He was ashamed of his sharecropping days. He told us, "You don't feel like a man when you work for someone else, while being forced to take the leftover crumbs. It is so demeaning. Walk tall, hold your head up, and never take what is not yours. Never sharecrop or rent. Always own your own home."

Those words resonated in each of our heads. All eight of us continued in school. I am so proud of all my brothers and sisters.

George, the oldest was drafted in to the military and became a Technical Sergeant. He volunteered as a Boy Scout Organizer. He received an Associate Degree and owned a large Laundry Mat and a ten bedroom home.

Maxine became a seamstress, a tax consultant and she bought her home with enough land to have a garden as large as Mama's.

Calvin spent many years in the Navy. He worked his way up to Aircraft Engineer. He owned his own home where he planted a garden. He bragged about his farm out back.

111

Crystal became a nurse and cosmetologist. Flowers and a gigantic garden surround her home, which is a mixture of vegetable and fruit trees.

Larry spent time in the Military and then worked at Kellogg's. Later, he was hired as Head of Security for a large company. His home had citrus trees and a garden.

Lynn became a nurse and a Mary Kay consultant. She owned her home also.

Dean the youngest served in the military. He attended college and became a great photographer and a Certified Carpenter. His home has a back yard with fruit trees and vegetables.

Mama and Daddy would be proud of all of us.

Thirst for Education

He that trusteth in his own heart is a fool:
but whoso walketh wisely, he shall be delivered.

Proverbs 28:26

Chapter 10
Jeanine Becomes Paraplegic

" Mother! Mother! Pamela hurt herself. She fell on a rock and it is stuck in her knee and she can't stand up. Come on," said Ellen.

I rushed to her and found her lying on the ground crying. I saw the rock stuck in her knee, closed up inside the skin. I wasn't sure how to get it out. I helped her into the car and took her to the emergency room and they pulled it out.

We returned home and Pamela still walked backward. "It hurts too much to bend it."

"You must walk normally. It will heal wrong if you continue to walk backward."

The phone rang. "Hello, Pierson residence."

"Mrs. Pierson? This is Mercy General Hospital. We have your daughter Jeanine here in the emergency room. Can you come down right away?"

"Yes. Thank you. I'll be right down." What now? "That was the hospital. Jeanine is there now and I have to go pick her up. I'll be back in a little while."

I pulled into the hospital parking lot expecting to just pick her up and bring her home. Someone must have contacted Al. I saw his car in the parking lot. This must be something bigger than I thought.

I entered the emergency room. After inquiring about my daughter, they led me to her. Jeanine lay on a gurney, unconscious and in a fetal position. Her face looked bluish her lips were puckered. Her hands lay folded beside her ears, like a newborn baby.

I turned to Al. "What happened?"

"They said she was in a car accident on the freeway." He looked worried. I knew he wasn't telling me something.

The doctor pulled back the curtain and walked up to the bed studying her chart. "Doctor, what is wrong with Jeanine? She looks fine, no blood or wounds anywhere on her body. Why does she look like that?"

The doctor gave me a grave look. "She has a broken back. All of her injuries are internal."

I couldn't believe he was so calm. "How will that affect her walking?"

"Oh, she will never walk again."

I burst out in uncontrollable screams. A nurse held me while I cried. How did this happen?

Al looked at me and said, "You shouldn't have bought her that car. It's your fault! If she didn't have the car she wouldn't have had an accident." He turned around and left the room.

I did not want to leave her. I stayed by her side. They just left her there, lying on that gurney.

"Do something, she must be in pain. Why is she just laying here? Help her. Help her, please! Why is she shaking like that?" I had so many questions that they didn't know how to answer.

The Doctor came in. "We are waiting for a back specialist to tell us what the next step should be."

I waited wanting to touch her, but where? My touch

may hurt her. I stayed by her side. It was after midnight when the nurse pleaded for me to go home. "You won't do her any good if you're exhausted. The best thing you can do for her right now is get some rest."

I did not say a word to Al when I got home. The nerve of him accusing me of causing Jeanine's accident. The pain in my heart swelled after I got into bed with Al. He never even tried to console me. I could not fall asleep so I got up and went back to the hospital.

Al had gone with me to get the car for Jeanine on the army base where Jerry was stationed. Jeanine was in her first year of college. Jerry found the car at a very low price because the owner was being deployed overseas and needed to get rid of it before shipping out.

We bought Pamela a car her first year of college. Not getting Jeanine a car wouldn't have been fair. They both wanted to stay home and attend a collage nearby. Catching the bus meant getting up before dawn some days. I didn't think that was safe. Al and I went to the army base together to check out the car. He never voiced his disapproval and I trusted his judgment about the car's condition.

I had a hard time accepting my daughters' predicament. I knew nothing about caring for a paraplegic. None of my children had ever been hospitalized. All of them were healthy, just the regular childhood diseases.

The days and years that followed this night took a toll on my life. Her accident happened a few months before my 48th birthday but I felt much older.

Jeanine was out of her head for about a week. She could not remember the accident. Jeanine endured forty-three back surgeries. Her second surgery put rods in her back enabling her to sit up.

117

She reverted back to a baby for a while. Whenever I left the room, she cried. She complained about how bad her legs hurt. We had not told her that she was a paraplegic. Her confusion was so great that we thought she would not understand.

"Mother will you please lift up my legs? They keep falling of the bed." I went to her bed and touched her legs. She expressed a sigh of relief, "Oh! That feels so much better."

The Doctor said, "In her mind she still thinks she can feel her legs."

A new era of my life opened before me. Everything I did now revolved around Jeanine. I gave up my life trying to save hers.

We insured the car she drove on the family policy. We employed an attorney to take care of the legal issues from her accident. We wanted her to be taken care of.

There was an investigation of the accident to determine fault--the driver of the eighteen-wheel, Hertz rental truck, or Jeanine in the Mazda she drove. I knew this would take some time so I focused my attention on Jeanine's recovery.

Four months later Jeanine had her eighteenth birthday. Without our knowing, she hired a lawyer herself. She thought things were moving too slow, and she wanted her money now. In her mind, she was going to get a million dollars from the accident. We had her covered but for not nearly that much.

The attorney said, "Jeannine is eighteen years old and viewed as an adult. She does not have to include you in any of her decisions. She chose not to employ the attorney you hired. She is of age to get her own and we will represent her. It's her choice."

I pleaded with her to wait, "You are too ill to make these decisions. You cannot know how much damage your body has and will endure. You should wait until you have a better idea of your future since the doctors are still performing all sorts of surgeries on you."

"I am eighteen years old and I know what I am doing. I can handle my own life."

Before her accident, Jeanine had left home to live with her boyfriend against our will. I had pleaded with her to wait until she turned eighteen. The boyfriend's grandmother signed for them to get an apartment near the college they were attending.

She still came home after school every day. The day of the accident, I was not there because I had taken Pamela to the hospital with the rock in her knee. It was raining when Jeanine took the freeway to her apartment.

The police report said that Jeanine's car went out of control, possibly because of the wet pavement. It spun across four lanes of traffic, hit the railing and bounced backed across all four lanes. Three cars had to brake to keep from hitting her. When she came to a halt, she landed in the path of an 18-wheel truck that ran over her car. She did not have a seat belt on and was thrown into the small cavity on the floor of the passenger side. Rescuers had to use the Jaws of Life to cut her out of the car. The truck flattened the steering wheel against the seat where she had been sitting.

Jeanine's life was never the same after that night. She became self-destructive and I became a slave to her commands. She had anorexia and I did not know it. I gained weight trying to get her to eat. I bought her anything she asked for. After taking one bite, she gave it me. I would describe how good it tasted to get her to try to eat more. I gained 30 pound in just a few months.

She only wanted me to attend to her hygienic needs and no one else. Jeanine spent six months in rehab and I was there every day to see her. I was in my final year of working on my master's degree. I had a hard time juggling classes and taking care of Jeanine. My main instructor lived near my house. She helped by allowing me to bring my assignments to her house instead of going across the Bay Bridge every day.

Jeanine was allowed to come home. Her friends came to visit. Some of them were not of good character. One of these young men took her out. I didn't know him. She had met him in a nightclub. There were times that I had to make him leave. He wanted to stay in her room all night.

She told him she was going to get a million dollar settlement. She had entwined herself in his life. When I realized he was hooked on heroin, he was not welcome in my home. He came anyway and was slow about leaving when I told him to get out.

The following year she got pregnant by this young man. How could this happen? I thought she was unable to bare children. Jeanine gave birth to a robust and healthy son. I felt like I had given birth to this child.

The baby's father would abuse her, often striking her for part of her welfare check. He said he was the father and deserved his part.

Jeanine got hooked on prescription drugs, and went on to heavy illegal drugs. I could not allow her to stay in my home. Her friends terrified me. The last straw was the day she shot at her sister.

Ellen did something Jeanine did not like. Jeanine picked

up an ashtray and threw it at her. Ellen threw it back.

"I will kill you, you almost hit my baby," she yelled.

Hearing the commotion, I entered the room. Jeanine searched in her purse and pulled out a pistol. She aimed it at Ellen and fired, missing her. I grabbed the gun out of her hand as she struggled to keep it. I slapped her out of her chair.

"But she was trying to kill my baby."

"And you were trying to kill my baby."

She left the house with her friends, taking the baby with her. I was concerned about the baby and sent someone to find her and bring the baby to me. He spent most of his life at our house.

Jeanine spent twenty-five years in her wheelchair. And so did I.

My Doctor, aware of what I was going through, recommended I enroll in an enabler meeting to learn how to practice tough love. I didn't get it. I could not see what the group was trying to get me to understand. My soft heart blinded me. I could not leave her in the dark when her lights were cut off. The babies needed milk and diapers I could not let them starve. I could not leave her sitting by the freeway when she ran out of gas.

After more babies arrived, I could not keep up the race. It was hard to care for seven children. Making sure they were enrolled in school, keeping up with their health problems and doing so many of the things she could not do because of her wheelchair.

I was so disappointed when Jeanine finally got her accident settlement. She had gone to her lawyers' office and asked for advances on her settlement. When she got her final payment, it was less than twenty thousand dollars.

I never could convince her that she sold herself short by not allowing me to help her get a bigger settlement. She paid ten thousand dollars for a big Lincoln Towne Car. She contacted a real estate agent and put five hundred dollars down on a one-bedroom house in a rundown area. It was a two-year interest only loan. The house cost twenty thousand dollars. She would not live in it herself.

I found her a tenant but the woman was mentally ill and I didn't know. Every week she called us and said the toilet seat was pinching her. She beat that seat until it broke. She would hit the ceiling with a broom until chunks fell to the floor. "I will not pay another penny until you fix everything right." We served her an eviction notice and she moved out.

I told Jeanine that she should sell her property before her interest only loan was due. She didn't understand what that meant. I found another real estate agent to help her get rid of the place. I had to get the place ready for the sale. I fixed the ceiling, replaced the toilet fixtures, landscaped the overgrown yard and painted the inside of the house.

Jeanine continued her unhealthy lifestyle. She gave birth to seven children, two of them born only eleven months apart. She spent most of her life in the hospital having one surgery after another. I pleaded with her to get her tubes tied.

Paraplegic Daughter

What man of you, having an hundred sheep,
if he lose one of them, doth not leave
the ninety and nine in the wilderness,
and go after that which is lost, until he find it?
And when he hath found it,
he layeth it on his shoulders, rejoicing.

Luke 15:4-5

Chapter 11
Sessy Divorces Alvin

Jeanine's illness put a strain on our already weak marriage. Al complained about me spending too much time with her and not enough time with him. He did not spend much time at home anyway. Ellen, our youngest would turn eighteen next year. I promised Mama that I would keep my family together until all the kids were grown. There was no way Alvin would leave the house and let me live in it in peace. My first shop was there and I didn't want to lose it, so it made sense that I should try to buy him out.

Like Mama always said, 'where there's a will there is a way'. So I made plans. First, I had to find a new shop. I had outgrown the location in the shopping center. Second, I needed a place to live. I was afraid to tell Al until I had it all figured out.

I truly believed that we hated each other. His life was at the church. He attended most of the activities and it didn't matter if he was the only male present. My life was with the kids and work. I went to all of their school activities and attended church with them on Sundays.

Ellen was our only child still under 18 years of age. I had tried so hard to assist her in getting a good education. All the children knew that I had planned to get a divorce when the time was right.

One of my clients at the salon was a real estate agent. "Hey Sessy, My boss is building a whole section of Town Houses near me and he asked me to help him sell them. You got all these customers here. Talk to some of them. I will pay you for any leads. How about that?"

"Girl, you know I will. But I will have to see them first."

"Sure, but they aren't finished yet. I'll take you whenever you have time."

The following week she took me to look at the development site. I was a little disappointed at the location. It was almost in the ghetto.

"Now, make sure you tell people the new town houses are good for the neighborhood. They upgrade the area. It's only five blocks from the new shopping mall, two blocks from the elementary school and about six blocks from the freeway," she said.

The more I learned about Town Houses the more enticing they became. "Girl, I don't think I will have any trouble selling them."

She took me to meet the developer. We seemed to hit it off right away. He was a Chinese gentleman who owned a high-class restaurant in China Town where the three of us had a joyful lunch. He said, "I have no doubt that you will be a good seller and make a lot of money. Better yet why don't you buy one before the price goes up?"

"Whoa, me? I don't have that kind of money! I wish I did."

"Just talk to your friend, our agent. She may come up with something that could work out for you."

My mind whirled a mile a minute. Could I really buy one of those Town Houses?

My friend, the agent, called me the next morning all bubbly and excited. "Girl, what did you do to my boss? He thinks you are a smart lady. He wants you to have one of the places. If you pick out one of the models that is not built yet you could start saving for the down payment. And if you are a little short he will lend you the balance and you could pay him back in installments."

"Why not? I need a place to live." Like Mama always said, 'where there is a will there is a way'.

The following week I signed the papers, locked in the price, and started saving for my new home. I could always sell the place and buy in another area. Doing better was my motivation to work hard and achieve my goals.

My nights felt longer. My nerves were getting the best of me. Have I taken on too much too fast? I gained weight very fast. I could not fasten my pants because of my fat stomach. It was time for my routine medical checkup.

My Doctor performed his usual procedures and discovered that I had a large fibroid tumor the size of a cantaloupe. Oh my God! That means surgery to remove it, and an interruption in my plans. I had planned to file for my divorce soon. The surgery would set me back.

My sister Crystal expressed concern for my recovery, "You shouldn't be climbing those steep stairs at your house after your surgery. If you want, come to my house for your recovery. It'll be fine."

While I waited for the surgery, I decided to obtain an attorney and file for divorce with the instruction to hold off on serving Al papers until I said to serve him. The attorney thought it didn't make sense to do it that way. He did not know that I was afraid to go home with Al there after he had been served the papers. I needed time to recover and then go home.

I left Pamela in charge of the beauty shop. She handled everything well until I was able to return.

The day that Ellen turned 18 years old, I called my attorney and told him to serve the papers.

I was still recovering at my sister's when Al came by to visit. He acted surprised and asked me why I filed these papers? I thought they were clear enough.

He never asked me to reconsider or tried to make things work out. His reaction was, "Sessy, I feel sorry for you. Some man is going to make a fool out of you. Don't come running back to me."

I made no reply. Why stir up a fire? There was no benefit.

I had to return home before the divorce was final. I moved upstairs in the room with Pamela.

The townhouse was still under construction. It was not moving fast enough for me. My friend, the real-estate agent, asked her boss to speed up the project if he could. They moved faster than I expected and my down payment was not ready. However, I did have most of it. The owner stayed true to his word and gave me a loan for the shortage. He gave me one year to repay him. I did it in seven months.

Pamela and I moved into the town house when it was finished, leaving Al and Ellen in the house in Berkeley. Ellen would not go to school or work. "If you get back in school or get a job I will take you with me," I said. She refused to do either.

Al lost control of the house. Ellen had too many friends visiting. Some of them rented rooms there. The place was filthy. Al locked himself in his room.

The court ordered us to sell the house and split the profit

fifty-fifty. Al swore he would not give me one red cent. He would make sure the house would never sell. Pam and I told Al that we found a real-estate agent and needed a date to show the house. We cleaned house the whole weekend. Al chased the agent away and advised him not to return. He did this again and again. I begged Al to let me buy him out.

"Never! I don't need you to buy me out. I will stay here until I die."

A few years passed. I waited and saved money to be able to redeem that house. I had worked at the cannery nights and fixed hair days to buy that house so many years ago. I believed God wanted me to keep it.

I asked Al to allow me to have the house appraised. We did not go through the cleaning this time. I told him that he should clean the place up before the appraisal. The house had lost over half its value.

I asked Pam to offer to buy her father's share. He was planning to move back to his parent's home because they were both deceased. He accepted her offer and I funded her buy-out. Thank God! I had regained the house that I had spent many nights working at the cannery to purchase.

After many repairs, we decided to rent it out, and put it in Section 8 care. It was nearly destroyed. They turned the garage into an auto repair shop, rented rooms to friends and kept the place filthy.

In the meantime, we searched for a bigger salon location.

Sessy Divorces Alvin

Thou hast granted me life and favor,
and thy visitation hath preserved my spirit.

Job 10:12

Chapter 12
Sessy's New Business Venture

The time had arrived to move up in the world, spread my wings as far as I could and seize the opportunity in front of me. I had outgrown the little shop in Berkeley. The walls were bulging. We had only been in business for four years. There was no space to hire more operators.

I began looking for a bigger building in a prime location. I bought magazines about how salons should look and what kind of services they offered. I got a general idea of what I wanted but I needed to see it firsthand.

I looked up the phone numbers of all the elite salons in the area, called for a manicure and kept my appointment.

"Oh boy! Just look at this place it would cost me a fortune to build."

I repeated this action for several months and got good ideas of what I could duplicate from the other salons.

My real-estate agent showed me many locations. Most of them were raunchy and in an unsafe neighborhood.

My cousin dropped by the shop one day and said, "Sessy I found you a shop. It's for sale, not for rent. I think you will like this one. What time do you get off? I'll come by and take you to see it."

Pamela and I followed him to the building after work. A dental manufacturing company had relocated to a larger facility. The building was ideal but the area was classified as the red light district.

Before I made a decision, I wanted to research the activities in the area. We drove by the building at all times of night and day and it was the red light district. A big church sat on one end of the block. A Planned Parenthood Clinic was across the street in front of us. Three Churches and a Funeral Home were on the other corner. Several rundown hotels were located on both sides of the street. A large flower shop sat a few doors down from us.

The good outweighed the bad. We were within walking distant from the BART train, near four hospitals and many of Doctors' offices. We had easy access to all four freeways and we could walk to the large shopping mall.

It was a one floor, free standing building with a parking lot that could handle twelve cars. Perfect. Just what we needed.

We purchased the building and the construction began. I started the legal part of the business. Forming a corporation, Internal Revenue Service, city business license, the Board of Cosmetology and all the legal action required to own a business.

We continued to work at the cramped location by day and spent our evenings and weekends at the new location getting it ready for a grand opening.

This time we could buy new equipment with the help of a salon designer to set it up. The place was so upscale it was hard for me to believe that we were the owners.

The front door opened to a reception area on one side and the resale area on the other. Four double-sided operator stations sat in the middle. To the right side was a tightly secured room made of a thick wall that the previous owners built to protect the Gold and Silver used in making dentures. Next to that, were four private rooms we used to shield the clients that did not want to be seen getting hair replacements. A full kitchen, inventory room and a meeting room sat in the back corner. On the opposite side were the shampoo area and manicure stations. The row of dryers, were positioned along the wall near the Pedicure stations. My office was very cozy. My son Larry computerized it and installed a sound system that played soft music throughout the salon.

It was almost time for the opening day. "Pamela, I think we should have two openings for this shop"

"Why two?"

"Well we do have a large clientele and we could honor them by inviting them to a V.I.P (very important patrons) day."

We set the date and sent invitations to every customer. We asked my brothers Larry, Calvin and Dean, to wear black Tie apparel and female hosts to wear after five dresses. The kitchen was loaded with finger foods and a wine fountain. The men stood at the door welcoming the customers, giving them a rose and ushering them to the lady greeters who gave them a tour of the salon.

The oos and ahs gave my heart such a boost.

The highlight of the day was when the city official cut the ribbon and welcomed us to the city.

Our salon was the only one called a Health and Beauty Salon. Our services expanded to the Hospital that needed help with patients who had lost their hair from burns or cancer. We became a vender for the cancer society and Medicare paid us to measure and fit them with breast prosthetics. We conducted free Seminars on how to take

133

care of the hair and nails using our product line. The San Francisco Chronicle featured us in articles praising us for our work in combating cancer.

Time brings about a change and everything has a cycle. In order to stay in business one must follow the trends and fads. Jerri curl started a new cycle. Instead of the client coming into the salon every two weeks, they only needed us every two or three months. Many shops closed for lack of work.

I added a new dimension by offering a gift certificate to our services, which was a big hit. We closed the shop on certain days and only certificate holders could come in. The operators looked special for this occasion. They worked together in teams.

The certificate stated, "Pamper your wife, mother or friend. This includes a Facial, Massage, Manicure, Pedicure and refreshments."

The shop was doing well. We were a Hair Replacement Center. I wanted to sell hair to my clients. I called venders from several states asking them to sell me wholesale packages. Two companies invited me to New York to work out a deal. Both deals fell through because they were not good offers. However, I did get a look at how they processed the hair. In order for me to build my own plant, OSHA would fine me on every corner. My trip to Florida was a little friendlier but I did not like their products.

Six months later, we had the Grand Opening at the Marriott Hotel, which was successful. Our clients modeled the latest hairstyles. Several clothing stores allowed us to use their lines to enhance the show. The Dance that followed was jumping.

We had clients coming from San Francisco, San Jose,

Richmond, Mill Valley, Walnut Creek and other cities in the Bay Area. I had dreams of expanding to another cite. San Francisco would be first because so many came from that area. San Jose would be our third location.

Nothing stayed the same. We began to have disturbances. Pilferage increased throughout the salon. Alcohol and drug made its way through some of the staff and operators. There was no way that I could leave the salon and open another location. I lost my desire and gave up on the idea.

The Town House I had bought was not the place that I wanted to live. Instead of the neighborhood getting better, it became worst. The little kids that used to ask to let them go to the store for me for twenty-five cents, were now teenagers and selling drugs next door to me. Drive-by shootings were common. Their customers would park in my driveway and would move when they got ready. The teenagers parked old cars in the lot to have something to duck under when the shooting started.

I wanted to move back to my house in Berkeley but it needed repairs.

I talked to the boys about the problems they were causing with their friends parking in my driveway.

One of them said, "You just let me know when they do that again I will bust a cap in him."

Of course, I did not tell him again. I was driving a Gold Cutlass Supreme. The boy next door bought a car just like My car. I went out of town for a weekend and put my car in my driveway to protect my house and the car. When I returned somebody had shot six holes in my car.

I moved back to Berkeley the following week and repaired the house while I lived there.

The house was now too big for me. I needed to do

135

something with all this space. When we were building the added rooms, it never occurred to me that I would be alone one day.

I decided to turn it into a duplex. I looked at the blueprints and put walls where there were doors. I turned the den into a kitchen, made the shop the living room and blocked off the door that entered into my part of the house. I left the bathroom where it was. I then rented it for the same amount of my loan payment, which was not too high for a one-bedroom apartment.

Jeanine was still having more babies. I went to visit her one day. Her stomach looked a little pouched out.

"Jeanine, please don't tell me that you are pregnant again."

"No I am not. How could I be pregnant when I am not doing anything? That's this colostomy bag I have to wear."

She shook it around and I fell for her answer. I had not noticed that she made her visits far and few between and most of them were by telephone.

One day I got a call from Dana her oldest daughter. "Nana, this is Dana we are at the Hospital."

"What are you doing at the hospital?"

"Momma is in here."

"What's wrong with her?"

"She just had a baby."

"What!" I couldn't believe it.

Dana said, "momma had the baby just a few minutes ago."

"Do you know what hospital she is in?"

"Yes," and gave me the name.

This was Jeanine's seventh child while living in a wheel chair. I was pretty upset with her. I had tried so many times to help her get her tubes tied. I was already working over-time trying to keep her kids in diapers, milk, food in their mouths and a roof over their heads.

The business was going well but my knees were tired of all the hours that I was putting on them. I began to walk with a limp. One evening after work, I found myself walking backward to the car. I drug myself under the steering wheel and headed straight to the hospital. The x-ray indicated that I needed surgery. The following week I underwent arthroscopic surgery on my right knee.

My job took a toll on my health and there was no way that I could cut back. I was working six days a week and attending church on Sundays.

I had hired three members from Al's family and six members from my family. Out of those nine people, no one showed interest in branching out, or running the original salon. I felt used up and lonely.

One of my male clients asked me if I was doing any dating.

"Heck no! When do I have time to think about dating?"

"You better take time girl. You are heading toward your fifties. After that it's a downhill roll."

He knew someone that he thought would be a good match for me, a workaholic like me. He was single and had never been married. After completing all the seminars that I had scheduled, I decided to meet this man.

Our first date was nice. He didn't intimidate me. He was so quiet and calm. In my mind that was good. I had no intention to do anything but occasional dating. He did not ask anything of me and did not try to stop what I was doing. I invited John on some of my business trips we both seemed to enjoy those events.

John informed me that he wanted to get married.

"No way! I do not ever want to get married again."

My business grew well. I added Student licensing to our service. Some of my relatives obtained their Cosmetology licensing under my tutelage. My marketing skills, through television advertising, were a big hit. Winning the Best Beauty Salon Award three years in a row, gave my shop the edge it needed.

New Business New Life

And he shall be like a tree planted by the rivers of water,
That bringeth forth his fruit in his season;
his leaf shall also not wither;
and whatsoever he doeth shall prosper.

Psalms 1:3

Chapter 13
Sessy Remarries

Eight years had passed since Al and I divorced. After being married to him for 32 years, I acted and felt as though I was still a married woman. I filled my life with work, church and the kids. I was hesitant because I didn't know how a good marriage worked. How could I love someone that I was afraid of and disliked?

John and I continued to date. He never pressured me in any way. He was easy to get along with and I liked the calmness that he brought to my life. He never married, nor had any children of his own. His mother lived with him and they were very close. I believed in the old saying, 'when a man is good to his mother he will be good to his wife.'

Our relationship grew stronger as time went by. We trusted each other. He helped me with my children and grandchildren. After five years of being almost inseparable, he started talking of marriage.

Of course, I wanted no part of it. I cared for him dearly but I got a glimpse of his family and how they felt about me. The rumors were horrible.

"John has a girl-friend who is as old as his mama and she has a whole bunch of grand kids."

He would say. "You don't have to worry about my family. You're with me not them."

141

However, I did worry. They seemed to know every move we made.

He had lied about his age. I knew he was a few years younger. When I saw his driver's license, I learned that he was nine years younger. I didn't think that qualified me as a cougar. Or did it?

John had been a bachelor all of his adult life and he didn't know what it meant to be a husband. The men in his family felt that a man should always have a mistress on the side. If he didn't, he was considered 'henpecked'.

John told me funny things about his uncles and cousins. They grew up in a rural area. The only place they had to meet their girlfriends was in the woods or behind buildings. John and his friend followed them to the woods and watched them.

One day his uncle caught his girlfriend with another man. He ran after her to beat her up but she fell over a log and broke her leg. He, being a gentleman, could not take her home to her husband. So he took her to a bridge and sat her over a broken board, her leg hanging through.

He screamed, "somebody help! Help! Help! Mandie's leg must have fallen through the crack. I found her like this. We better hurry before a train comes and kills her."

John's father had two families. His mother had seven children and lived in the rural area. His girlfriend had eight children and lived in the city. He didn't take care of any of them.

John's sisters went to school because his Mama felt that they needed an education. The boys had to quit school and take care of the family. Their family migrated from Alabama to California in the 1960's. All the boys got jobs of some sort but John was the one that took care of his

Mother.

The family had no secrets from each other. They fought amongst themselves and never let anyone else enter their tight circle.

Hard times, mistreatment and lack of education had left a blanket of mistrust over his mother's life. She felt it her duty to look out for her children. She told her boys "I am the boss of this house. I taught you how to work and have something. You work and bring your check to me. I will put it away so none of those low down women can take it away from you."

John and I took trips together. He experienced his first Cruise with me and we had a ball. He spent more time at my house than with his mother. He accompanied me on business trips and other places.

He kept pushing for marriage. But I held on to staying single.

"Look Sessy, I really want to get married. I am tired of being a bachelor. All my friends are married. I don't know why you're so afraid. We do get along. You have the brains and I have brawn, together we could do well. At least give it some thought."

Another year went by I came to depend on his daily presence.

Illness struck again. My left shoulder needed surgery. I tore my rotator cuff. John took a week off from work to take care of me. I was so flattered by his action.

I started to add thing up. The good things about John outweighed the bad. Plus, he had become a big part of my life. I could hardly wait for him to ask me to marry him again.

He asked me in a strange way. "Sessy, I am tired of

waiting for you to marry me. I know you are concerned about my family and how they feel about you. Forget that. I told you, you are not marrying them, you will be marring me. I don't always get along with all of them myself, so come on let's get married."

"John I have thought about it. We do care about each other. I see no reason to say no again. Let's get married."

He was adamant about not having a big wedding. He said that was such a waste of money that could be used for things we needed.

We decided to have a private wedding and a reception in the garden of my home. The staff from the salon hosted the party. A few of his family members attended the event. His mother and sisters were invited but decided not to attend.

Our marriage started out well. We had reached our comfort zone. John did not try to change me and I did not try to change him.

His mother made it clear that she would still do his cooking. He left my house every morning to have breakfast with her and pick up his lunch pail on his way to work. I was okay with that. I had cooked for many years, and if that's what he wanted, go for it.

John was overweight and had high blood pressure. I asked him to go with me to a health fair and get a free vital check. His blood pressure was very high and his cholesterol level was over 300.

I showed him that all of my results were good. "It is the food that you eat every day that is causing the problem. If you would like, I can prepare your food when I prepare mine. You will feel better in the long run."

He agreed but he lied to mother. He told her, "The

doctor told me that I need to eat different to lower my blood pressure and cholesterol level I can eat only fruit so I will pick that up myself."

I replaced the two fried pork chops and biscuits with whole grain bread, chicken sandwiches, fruit and a surprise goody that I know he liked. His gourmet lunch pail was the envy of the other workers.

His mother did not like what I fixed even though his cholesterol level dropped 27 points the first month. He allowed her to examine his lunch pail and she wanted me to know that she had added her touch to his lunch. If I put in a banana, she would put in an orange. If I used plain paper towels, she would take it out and put flowered towels. I ignored the situation because I did not want a fight.

John and I never fought. Whenever I got angry with him, he would say, "Oh Let me get out of here. I will be back when you cool off."

"John we should clear things up. Walking off is not the answer."

He didn't know how to express his feelings. We had a lot of respect for each other but the love started to diminish. He was a good man and tried to treat me well. But he missed his bachelor days and started seeing other women. He hid it from me. When I found out, he denied it. That started the rift between us.

Sessy Remarries

Marriage is honourable in all, and the bed undefiled:
But whore-mongers and adulterers God will judge.

Hebrew 13:4

Chapter 14
Suicide in the Family

John called the salon and said, "Sessy, you need to come home right now." "Why? What's wrong?"

"You need to come home right now."

"Did something happen to Jerry?" I asked, the panic rising in my chest.

"Yes. He tried to kill himself. I have already called an ambulance."

I quickly assigned an operator to finish my client and told Pamela to reschedule all of my clients that would fit into her schedule. I rushed home as fast as I could. I made it there a few minutes before the ambulance arrived. Jerry had pulled his car into the garage, hooked a hose to the exhaust pipe and started the car with the opposite end of the hose to his nose.

It was a miracle that John arrived home earlier than usual. I know that God was in the plan that day. It was not time for my son to leave. Jerry was the quiet one who always hid his feelings. I knew he had been struggling ever since he lost his family five years before.

Jerry and Sung-Ja had two children while he was in the military before their marriage failed. Their final tour was in the state of Texas. Jerry did not re-up after his discharge.

They purchased a home there and Jerry began working as a computer analyst and lab technician.

Jerry started to drink heavily and made bad choices.

Sung-Ja had sent to Korea for her brothers to move in with her. They protected their sister, as most brothers' feel is the right thing to do.

Going to visit his kids had become a problem for Jerry.

During a visit, Sung-Ja's brothers threw him out. Jerry retaliated by returning and running his car through the den area of the house. He was arrested and went to jail.

He became angry at his situation and started having problems at his job. Charged with theft from his workplace, he was convicted and sent to prison.

He wrote me a long letter trying to explain what happened to him. I realized I was only hearing one side of the story and encouraged him to make a new start and always be there for his children.

Jerry called me from prison. "Mother, I can't stand it in here anymore. Please. Is there any way you can help me? Get me out of here."

"I want to help you but you gotta be honest with me. What really happened? Why were you really incarcerated? Tell me the truth now."

"I am in here because my job said that I stole one of their computers. I did not steal it. I took it home to finish some work that needed to be done I was taking it back when they stopped me."

He gave me the name of his attorney. I contacted the man. He told me he wasn't sure where the case stood but Jerry owed him $700.00. If I could send him that amount, he would let me know soon.

When Jerry called again, I informed him of the money

that I had paid.

"What? I didn't owe him any money. Call him and ask for your money back."

I called and left messages, never getting an answer. I wrote a letter and it was returned.

Just thinking about my son being in a Texas prison took a toll. My imagination ran away with me.

A call from Jerry nearly pushed me over the edge. "Mother please try to get me out of here. I just saw them beat a man to death. I am so scared. Please Mother."

"What on earth can I do?" I had no idea where to start.

Jerry told me about a black female parole officer that he had met.

He gave me her number. I called her and she lashed into me. "Why do you mothers go to great length to get these kids out of trouble? He got himself in this trouble let him get himself out."

"Please help me. This is his first time in jail."

"I will not promise you anything. Give me your number and I will get back to you. Don't call me, I'll call you."

She called me about a week later to inform me that I should assure her that he would have a job, a place to live and meet his assigned parole officer. "As soon as I receive this information you will hear from me."

I set about making the arrangements and got her the information as fast as I could.

The long wait ended. The call from Texas was good news. "Listen to me Miss Sessy, I will help you this time but if that boy gets into trouble again you let him get himself out."

"Oh thank you, thank you, and May God bless you for all of your help."

When Jerry arrived home, I was surprised at his weight loss. "Boy you better start eating to put some weight on. I plan to work the hell out of you at the beauty shop."

He gave a half ass smile and said, "I am not afraid of work I am just so glad to be home. I can take some of the pressure off you. Thank you so much Mother I will make it up to you, you will see."

Jerry worked hard at computerizing the business. He cooked most of the meals at home and did all the laundry.

Something about Jerry was changing. I could not put my finger on it but he began to act out of character. He started going back to the salon at night. His excuse was, "I need to work on the computer to finish some stuff."

"Why can't you do it tomorrow?"

"I won't be long." But he stayed all night.

I just assumed that he was experiencing depression because of the loss of his family.

He dated one of the customers at the salon. She was a nice young lady. When he moved in with her, they seemed happy.

This was the beginning of the end. She told me he was involved in the drug world. After she ended their relationship, he got his own apartment. I rarely saw him.

One day he appeared at my door looking thin but clean and neatly dressed. "Jerry what's wrong with you? You look a mess. I don't mean your dress I mean your face and your skinny body."

"Mother I am alright. I just need a good job. I came by to see if you could give me a care package of food. I don't have food in my apartment I ran short this month. What do you have cooked?"

"You know I keep food in my house. Get what you see

in there."

I gave him items that he would have to cook. Red beans, rice, frozen meat, grits, seasoning and a few other items.

I did not see him again for a while. His next visit was for another care package. I asked him if he was seeing his parole officer on time.

He said, "Yes I am."

"Listen Jerry, from your looks there is something wrong. You need to be up front with me."

"There is nothing wrong with me."

"If you get into any trouble you are on your own. I will keep my word. You get into trouble you get out yourself."

Jerry was at the employment office waiting in line when he passed out on the floor. He called me at home and told me of his predicament. "Can you pick me up?"

"Yes. If you can walk to the Beauty shop, I will meet you there."

He was waiting on the steps. I gave him a big hug and said, "Let's go and get something to eat at the fast food place across the street."

He ordered what he wanted.

"Let's go eat in the car." I knew that he would have to listen to what I had to say. You cannot get a message to a hungry person because the stomach takes precedence.

"Jerry, you know that I am aware that you have a drug problem?"

"Yes. I was ashamed to admit it to you."

"I know of a place that you can go for rehab. I have already talked to them but only you can do it for yourself. They want you to call them and make an appointment. I can't go with you. You have to do it on your own. I will give you bus fare when you are ready and you should do it

151

soon. Like, tomorrow."

"Yes. I will. Can I stay at your house tonight?"

"Sure. Then you'll be near the bus line and get there early."

Jerry boarded the bus at 8:00am. He checked in and was told to sit on a bench until someone came to get him. He said they ignored him the entire day. Still he waited for them to come.

He was called in for his interview and they told him he had been accepted. He was given a week to go home and get all of his business finalized and then return to stay for two years. It would be one month before he could contact anyone. "Bring only the clothes on your back and nothing else."

Family day arrived and we were invited to have dinner with our loved ones. It had been over a year since I had seen Jerry. We wrote letters back and forth to keep in touch.

John and Pamela attended the dinner with me. We checked in and were told that Jerry was in the yard greeting the families. We did not see him and asked for help to find him.

A young man said, "There he is right there."

"I don't see him." I looked around but still didn't know which one was him.

He pointed and said, "Right there."

I was shocked! This well dressed smiling young man looked at me. His skin was a few shades lighter and he was at least twenty-five pounds heavier.

"Jerry, look at you. You look great. I did not recognize you."

The dinner was formal and tasty. Our visit came to a close. I left feeling grateful that my son had been spared the dreadful life of drug abuse.

Jerry stayed an extra year. He became a music teacher, a computer instructor and a trusted escort that would take individuals home for visits. He trusted himself and accepted a job at Kaiser Hospital. The job was through the rehabilitation center where he resided. This job took six of their students, six months to complete.

Jerry's duty was to build an inventory database. The hospital had a warehouse full of over five thousand pieces of equipment that could not be located when needed. Jerry alphabetized and identified every item. He created software and had planned to use the software to get a job at other businesses.

The rehab establishment said the software belonged to them. He grieved about not getting one cent for all that work. They were paid very well for his work.

Jerry started looking for work outside the program. His resume looked good but his prison and drug record put a damper on everything that he had going for him.

He finally landed a job at the V.A hospital as a lab technician. This job really depressed him because of low pay and the unclean conditions the patients had to endure.

We were invited to a big family picnic. I invited Jerry to go with me. Many of his cousins were there and some of them had not seen him in years. He did a lot of talking with them, which was unusual for him.

His uncle teased him about becoming so talkative. "Boy, I use to try to make you talk. When you said hi you had talked your ass off." They both had a good laugh.

Jerry went to my house while I was at work. I did not realize it but he had given away some of his things, including a computer, to a teenager next door.

The following week the Berkeley police came by and John answered the door. They asked John if he knew Jerry and he said no.

"Does Jerry live here?"

"No, he doesn't."

As he closed the door, I asked, "Who was at the door John?"

"It was the police looking for Jerry, I didn't know what was going on and I told him that he did not live here."

"I wish you had told me. I think he may be missing because the rehab center called me looking for him also."

I went to work feeling sad. I knew something was wrong, but could not put my finger on just what it was. The day seemed long and heavy. My receptionist and I were the last to leave that evening. I burst into tears and could not explain why.

She tried to console me, "What's wrong? I've never seen you act like this before?" She gave me her phone number and told me to call her no matter what time, day or night.

The police returned the following night and I answered the door. "We need to talk to you Ma'am." He showed me his badge and asked if he could come inside for a minute.

"What's this about?"

He asked me to sit down. "Do you know Jerry?"

"Yes he is my son, is something wrong?" I began to shake.

"We found his body hanging from a tree behind U C Berkeley University. It does not seem to be foul play. We are still investigating the situation but all the evidence points to suicide."

My whole world seemed to turn black. The officer

asked if I was alone. Luckily, someone was at home. He said they would leave and come back in a few days. "Here is my card if you wish to call for any reason. Sorry for your loss."

"Thank you."

I informed my receptionist of what had happened.

She responded by saying, "That is why you were crying the other day. It was God's way of telling you that something had happened to your child."

Why didn't I see that he was suffering? He did not show any signs of ending his life. He left a note pinned on the calendar when he tried to asphyxiate himself in the garage. This note read:

"Do not cry for me. I died five years ago. What you see now is an old shell. I do wish that we could have one more fish dinner."

He did not like fish. I could not understand why he would say such a thing.

The days that followed were hectic. My tears seemed to have an everlasting flow that I could not cut off.

The rehab facility offered their condolences. A busload of his friends from the center came to bid farewell to Jerry. Some of his close friends from there wanted to take part in the funeral services. His music students performed beautifully. The President spoke well of him and expressed sorrow for his loss.

Jerry's death left a hole in my heart that only God could heal. It was evident that he had planned to do this long before that day. As I was going through his belongings, I discovered two small insurance policies. One was to me and the other was to his daughter. The one to me was just enough to cover his funeral.

The guilt that yanked at my soul was so painful. I am his mother. Why had I not seen the pain that he was feeling? He had promised Tony and me that he would never try suicide again. I believed him. I would have done almost anything to let him know that he was loved and his life was worth living.

Suicide in the Family

Blessed are they that mourn: for they shall be comforted.

Matthew 5:4

Chapter 15
Alvin passes away

A lvin had a heart attach the same week that my father died. Pamela and I went back to Mississippi to attend the funeral and visit Al in the V.A. Hospital in Jackson Mississippi.

My father, Jim, lived to be 95 years old. He was an active man who went shopping for himself, did his own cooking, and cared for his much younger wife. He used a walker to steady himself. On his way to the bathroom, he got his walker caught up in an old throw rug that his wife put on the floor in the bathroom. His head hit the wall causing an injury that rendered him mute but alert. He lived about a month before passing away.

After his services, we went to visit Al. It had been a long time since I had seen Al. He had not yet been diagnosed with Alzheimer at that point but the signs were there.

When I greeted him he was very sick, yet he told me he was doing real well. "I have not felt better in my life." He survived the heart attack and was able to go home.

He still resided in his family home, alone. He soon became unable to care for himself. His brother lived a few miles away and would come and check on him almost daily.

One day Alvin's sister called me from Chicago. "Sessy

somebody needs to go and get Al. He is in bad shape. He's not eating well. I know that you have remarried and can't take him in but see if some of the kids will take care of him."

I called Tony our youngest son and explained the situation.

"Oh mother, I can't afford airfare for Daddy or me. I will go get him if you help with the fare."

I agreed and helped with all of the travel arrangements "Your Daddy should have some of the money that he got from the sale of our house."

I gave Tony Alvin's other sisters phone number. When he changed planes in New Orleans, he called her to inform her of his visit.

"Call me when you arrive," she said.

He had a long layover and wanted to visit his aunt while he was there. "Hi auntie I am at the airport now can you come and pick me up?"

"Oh yes, son, I will be there in a few minutes to get you."

He waited for hours and she never showed up or called him. He arrived in Mississippi and called his uncle to pick him up at the bus station.

Alvin recognized him and was happy to see him. "Boy what are you doing here?"

"I came to see about you, Daddy. How are you doing?"

"Well the old man is doing alright. How long are you planning on staying?" Al asked.

"I was worried about you so I come to get you and take you home with me."

"I don't know about that. I better stay here."

"Daddy you are alone in this house you could have

160

another heart attack," Tony said. "Just stay with us a little while and if you don't like being at my house I will bring you back."

"Well I guess so."

Tony settled any business that he could for his father. While going through his father's paper work Tony discovered that a woman posing as his caretaker had stolen all of Alvin's money leaving him $35.00. All his money from the sale of the house was gone. She knew that Al had Alzheimer's and took advantage of him by stealing all of his money.

Tony was furious with the bank. Why would they allow someone to cash a $500.00 check a day until it was all gone?

She had Al sign every check in the entire book and then kept the book. "This way I will not have to bother you when I do your shopping." She vanished when she realized his son was there.

Tony reported her. This was her livelihood--finding senior's and duping them for their saving's. She was later sent to prison for a long time.

The bank made excuses. Al signed the checks and that tied their hands. There was nothing the bank could do. Tony and Al were ready for the plane trip home.

After an hour or so on the plane, Alvin asked, "Jerry, how long is this tour going to take?"

"Not long Daddy and I am Tony, not Jerry. Did you forget that Jerry is dead?"

"Nobody told me."

"Yes. I called you and Mother called you."

Alvin became restless, "How much longer is this tour? I am fixing to get off right now."

"Daddy you can't get off the plane now we are still in

the air."

Alvin unbuckled his seatbelt and said, "Watch me," and started walking down the aisles.

Tony ran to catch him and guided him back to his seat. Alvin nodded off to sleep and was peaceful the rest of the trip.

Ling-su, Tony's wife, was very kind to Alvin. She took care of him, kept him clean and well fed. She found an adult care center operated by her friend. She dropped him off on her way to work and picked him up on the way home.

I know this was a big job for her. I would go to their home some weekends, prepare food and package it for the freezer so she would not have to cook every day.

Alvin's condition became worse. He started leaving the house and getting lost.

Tony informed the Police of Alvin's condition and gave them all the numbers that they could call if they ever found him. He never ran off in the day because he had what the Doctors called Sundowners Alzheimer's--they get more confused after the sun goes down.

One day Tony called me, frantic. "Mother, Daddy is in the Hospital."

"Slow down Tony what happened?"

He started crying and said, "He had several heart attacks."

"Do you want me to come?"

"He is still in the hospital I will call you when I talk to the doctor."

A few hours later Tony called. "He is dead Mother. He is dead and I don't know what to do."

"Calm down and let us make plans. You know we have to make funeral arrangements. Do you want me to come?"

162

"Not yet. I need to think. Will you start making some kind of arrangements and let me know what you come up with?"

I suggested that cremation would be a good option.

"Oh no, I do not want to burn Daddy up."

"Okay, okay that was just an option. I plan to be cremated when my day comes. So don't think of it as burning me up. My body will just be the shell where my soul used to dwell. There is nowhere in the Bible that say it is a sin. Only my ashes will go back to the earth."

Tony lived in Monterey and I lived in Berkeley almost two hundred miles away. I made plans to have the services in Berkeley where he had family, and a host of church friends. He was buried in a military cemetery in Pacifica California.

Alvin Passes Away

One generation passeth away, and another generation
cometh: but the earth abideth for ever.

Ecclesiastes 1:4

Chapter 16
John Returns to Bachelorhood

John showed signs of unrest. He had no complaints. He would say. "I have a good wife. You are the first lady that I have gotten along with for this long."

And I would reply, "I have a good husband. Thank you for bringing some happiness into my life."

Some of his family had finally accepted me, but the most of them did not. I was not lonely for friends but I preferred to be part of his family. "Oh well it's their loss not mine."

"John, I think I will skip church today."

"Why? You should continue doing what you did before we got together. Just because I don't go to church don't mean you should stop."

"I will always attend church on Sunday. It's just that we haven't spent enough time together. We should just stay home and enjoy the day or go somewhere that's fun for the both of us."

"Maybe next Sunday. I promised my brother that I would visit him today. Some of his friends will be over there. You do not know them."

"Okay. I will see you later." I decided to stay home alone. Maybe watch movies, read a book, work puzzles, or just do nothing.

After dinner, I watched a long movie. I heard John returning and pretended to be asleep because I knew he would be drunk or pretend to be.

"Hey Sessy. You 'sleep? Hey baby, Daddy's home. I guess you are asleep."

It was so hard to continue living like this, why did I pretend that I wanted to give us another chance. John had requested that we see a marriage councilor before we through in the towel. I knew when I saw his car parked in his old girlfriends backyard that our marriage was over.

John missed his bachelor lifestyle and he was afraid that he would be labeled henpecked.

I began to feel like a complete idiot. I had lost all my trust in him. His family was his life. Everything that went on in our house he ran by them to get their opinion on how to react to the problem.

"John do you remember what the marriage counselor told us?"

"Yes, some of it. I forgot most of it."

"My biggest complaint about our marriage is that you visit your family daily but complain when I visit my wheel chair bound daughter. There are so many thing she cannot do in that chair. Every Sunday I sit at home alone. All I asked from you was for you to spend two Sundays with me and two Sundays with your family. You agreed that was fair. I get home about noon from church. You have all morning to visit your family."

I tried to keep my word about the reconciliation.

The final straw that broke the camel's back arrived. He was to spend the day with me. I made a special dinner for us.

He announced that he was going to 'make a little run'.

"John, where are you going? And for how long?"

He gave me an ugly look. "Sessy, I am a grown man. I do not have to tell you where I am going."

"The only reason I asked is because I was getting ready to put the steaks under the broiler and I needed to know if I should wait until you return. I know that you are a grown man. Okay if that's the way you want to live."

"I do not have to tell you where I am going. You can do what you want with those steaks."

I never included him again in my Sunday dinners. I ate out or just fix dinner for myself.

I began to build a life without John. I made plans to get myself back on track.

After that last Sunday episode I informed John that I was not happy with our marriage and we needed to either fix it or get a divorce.

"If you want a divorce go ahead and get a lawyer. I will pay for it. I did not ask for a divorce. That's what you want," he said.

"I was thinking about going to City Hall and filing the papers myself. It's called a Marriage Dissolution, not a Divorce but it means the same thing." I gathered the proper papers with the intention of filing them when he was home to agree to the terms but I got caught up in getting the taxes for the shop prepared.

After a few days John asked, "Sessy, did you file the papers yet?"

"Not yet. I am trying to get all the employee W2 forms finished. I have the papers but just haven't had the time to fill them out yet. I thought you should be here when we fill them out. We should agree on all terms."

He spoke with anger in his voice. "Don't worry about

the papers. I will do it myself I just want to get it over with."

How could he do it himself? His reading and writing abilities were limited. Was this his way to stall or was he in a big hurry to get back to his bachelor days?

John continued to make his 'little runs'. One day he shocked me. He gave me an angry look and said, "Sessy, you better get yourself together."

"Okay what did I do? How do you mean that?"

"You know what I mean. Just get yourself together." He never did make it clear what he meant.

I really wanted to know what kind of ladies he was dating. Most of them were friends to his family. All I had to do was ask the friendly ones to tell me who they were. They were heavy drinkers and I realized that they made John feel important and he was in his comfort zone.

I later learned that one of his ladies had prepared the divorce papers for him.

I asked him, "What did I do to cause the failure in our marriage? I don't want to reconcile but I need to know so that I won't take the same thing into another marriage if I should decide to do so."

"Sessy, you did not do anything wrong. It was me I just did not want to tell you. I have not met a better woman. But, there were times when I was out that I did not want to come home. I have been accustomed of going places and staying three or four days. I knew that you would be hurt if I did that. And I did not know how to tell you that I needed my freedom. I was just being a man, that's all."

"John you do not have to wait for the divorce to be final. You should run to your freedom now." He packed his clothes and left.

He came by every day to pick up his mail. Even after I made an address change, he still came by. He started coming odd hours of the night. I had the locks changed and he could not understand why.

One night he rang the doorbell at 2:30 am. I looked through the peep hole in the door and asked him what he wanted. "Sessy, I need to lay down I am too drunk to drive home just let me sleep it off on the couch." I opened the door and he staggered in and fell on the couch.

I covered him with a blanket and went upstairs and locked my door. I was sound asleep when I heard the doorknob jiggling. It was John. "Sessy open the door. I can't believe you locked me out. Let me in."

"John you said if I let you in you would not give me any trouble. I have no intention of opening the door." "Come on Sessy. Open the door."

"If you don't get away from here I am going to call your mother and tell her what you are trying to do to me." "What did you say?"

I repeated in slow motion, "If-you-don't-get-away-from-my-door I am going to call your mother and to tell her what you are trying to do to me."

The sound of John's feet running down the stairs like a scolded dog was all I heard after that.

I chuckled. Does he think he can out run a phone call? I can't believe he tried to include me into his stable. Not with all the incurable diseases floating around. We are over... real over.

He began driving by my house and calling me later to ask whose car was parked in my driveway.

"What are you doing now?" he asked.

"I am cooking dinner, why?"

"Can I come have dinner?"

"Heck no, I have a guest for dinner."

"I am coming by to see who you have over there. You are still my wife until the divorce is final," he said.

"It's none of your business. Don't you dare come over here." My guest was the Shaklee lady that supplied my vitamins but I would not dare tell him.

In order to put a stop to this, I decided to attend a single's dating dance for professionals. I put on my best outfit and drove to Pleasanton about twenty miles away. It was at a high class hotel and I felt safe. I stood on the wall to watch how the others were acting. I really wanted to dance but no one asked me. I busied myself at the refreshment table. I will just get full and go home. This is not for me.

While I was chunking down cheese, crackers and cookies a young, well-dressed man came over and spoke to me. He told me his name which I could not pronounce. He shook my hand and asked me my name.

"Would you like to dance?"

"Sure."

We went into action but neither of us could dance. He was from Kenya, South Africa and had not learned any American moves. It had been years since I had been to a dance my steps had turned to stumps.

We decided to get to know each other.

He was an engineer in Silicon Valley and lived in the Valley. I asked him his age and he told me.

I let out a big belly laugh. He was my son's age. "Okay we've had a good time but it's time for me to go home before my glass slipper falls off."

"Wait Sessy. I want your phone number." He slipped his hand in his pocket and gave me his business card.

170

I lied and said that I had forgot to bring mine. "I will call you."

"No you won't. Please give me your number and I will call you. I would like to see you again."

I smiled and said, "Listen Mr. I can't say your name and I am twice your age. You should stay and try to find someone your own age. There is too much of an age difference. I was looking for someone older."

He walked me to my car still pleading for my phone number.

John kept calling trying to keep up with me. I got this bright idea, maybe I should call Mr. Kenya. It would let John know that he had been replaced. I don't have to get serious with him.

One Sunday John stopped by my house and Mr. Kenya answered the door. I introduced them. They both got upset.

Mr. Kenya said in a disappointed voice, "Your ex should not be coming by here anymore."

John called the next day and said, "Sessy who was that little short African at your house. I started to come back over there and blow his brains out. He had the nerve to ask me to leave."

"Listen to me John, I was trying to be civil to you, but you are taking this too far. You are not my husband any more. I am making a life for myself which does not include you. So go on with your life. You are free. Enjoy that freedom."

Mr. Kenya became too possessive and I broke off the relationship. He had served his purpose.

I broke all ties with John. I avoided him for a year. When I saw him again he had lost sixty pounds and looked much older and tired. He still lived with his mother and continued to try to play the field. Most of his girlfriends were deceased--at least four of them.

A few years later we became friends. He expressed his sorrow for our breakup and still blamed his family for their intrusion.

"John, don't blame them. If you had not told them everything that went on in our house they would not have had so much power."

Now John seems like a cousin to me. My family always accepted him.

John Returns to Bachelorhood

Thou shall not commit adultery.

Exodus 20:14

Chapter 17
Retiring and Relocating

My second marriage had come to an end. We both had our reasons. Now the time for me to make a new start lay before me. I'd had all the freedom I could handle. I needed to reach out and start all over. I felt good about myself after mourning the loss of my husband.

I wanted to go to a different part of the world. I felt adventure--something out there calling me. "At my age, I should be able to do any darn thing I want to do." I was not ready for the 'Bone Yard'. "Let's see what I can do to improve myself?"

Tony was stationed at Fort Ord military base where he met other veterans selling items that they could not take with them. "Hey Mother, I have a friend that has a car that looks like you. He is selling it dirt-cheap and it looks like new. He inherited it from his Mother who passed away. She rarely drove it. He is being deployed out of the country and can't take it with him. It's a Jaguar--a bad one Mother. I'll send you a picture of it. I know you will like it." He sounded so excited.

This may be one way for me to improve myself. After all, my old dodge was getting old. This would be an upgrade.

Tony was right. I did fall in love with the gun metal blue Jaguar. It was a little pricey but I jumped at the chance to drive that car.

"Tony, don't ever say the price was dirt cheap. I paid an arm and a leg for this car. Thank you for finding it for me." "You deserve it Mother."

"I must admit I got a new attitude."

The business was doing well but I was feeling so burned out. I felt like I was on a treadmill going non-stop every day. Why was I working so hard? Will there ever be an end to this madness that I once called a joy? At sixty-eight years old, I compared myself to a hamster making tracks and getting nowhere.

One of my clients in the salon suggested I meet her father. She thought we had a lot in common. He lived back east but visited her in the cold months. "He will be here next month I want you to meet. He is a health nut like you, has a beautiful home and is searching for a good companion."

I had planned to meet him. But Jeanine was having serious medical problems at the time of his visit. I did not find time.

He returned the following year. His daughter reminded me of his arrival and begged me to try to meet him this time.

We made plans to meet at the train terminal near my house. We described ourselves on the phone in order to find each other.

He said, "I am a dark skinned Haitian man wearing a brown suit, tan scarf and my hair is snow white with a matching mustache."

Oh boy. I would not have any trouble finding him.

"I will be waiting near the exit platform. Look for a

brown-skinned not very tall African American women. I will be wearing a purple floral head wrap and a matching top."

We went to dinner, had a great time and got to know a little about each other. Our friendship continued. We talked on the phone after he returned home. He invited me to come and visit him, and I accepted because I was looking for a different place in the world to take root for my final days.

His home was very neat and clean not one thing out of place. He prepared candlelight dinners with good wine. I was not allowed to do anything. I pinched myself to see if it was really happening to me. "Yep, it's me." He made me feel like a Queen.

I returned home and continued working at the salon, making plans to retire. I had never felt so burned out.

My Haitian friend showed himself when he came to visit me that winter. He hated my grandchildren. Came to the Salon and tried to take over. He would get mad if he thought I was late getting off.

I took him to the airport, dropped him curbside and did not look back. That's the last time I saw him.

I knew now, after that episode, that I would not be going to the east coast but continued to pack without a destination in mind.

One night I cried myself to sleep because I felt like a lost child alone in the wilderness. The next morning I jumped up and sat on the side of the bed. "I am moving to Las Vegas. That's where I am going, to Vegas. Yes Vegas."

I had read in the newspaper that the cost of living was less expensive and the homes were larger and more beautiful. The search was on. I found a good Real Estate Agent in Las Vegas. She sent me photos of eight houses to

177

see before I arrived. I narrowed it down to four. I repeated this for eight months until I found my dream home.

Getting the shop ready for sale was quite a job. We found a buyer that wanted to turn the Salon into a chocolate factory. Most of my clients were devastated by my retirement.

"Girls, I've gotten old. I will be seventy in a few years. I'd like to know what it feels like to sit on it for a while."

Pamela and Ellen relocated also. The three of us cleaned the house in Berkeley and put it up for sale. We split the furniture between us. Pamela moved to Oakland, Ellen moved to Fresno and I was moving to my new home in Henderson, Nevada.

Jeanine was in the Hospital.

We finished cleaning the house and realized we had bubbles in our throats. The girls were all born there. The sentimental memories made them fight back tears. We did our final walk through and we all broke down and cried like babies.

We joined in a group hug and I began to pray. "Lord, we thank you for giving us a chance to say goodbye to the house that gave us comfort for so many years. We thank you for giving all of us a chance to move on to other destinations and start our lives over again. Please keep us all safe and continue looking out for one another."

Ellen prayed a sincere prayer that made all of us cry even more.

Pamela kept crying.

I said, "Come on Pamela It's your turn."

"Oh I can't, I just can't."

We bundled up the kids—I had five of Jeanine's

children—and went to the hospital to say goodbye to her.

Jeanine cried so much. She worried the kids would not remember her—that she would never see them again. Her baby was only five but he had spent most of his life with me.

Our trip was delayed and we had to get a hotel room for a few days. Two of the kids got sick with high fevers. I took them to the hospital. One had the flu and the other had pneumonia.

We finally were able to start on our trip to Nevada. It was raining and cold that December. Driving was a pain in the neck. I had a hard time staying awake because the sick kids had kept me up.

We finally made it home. Alvin's nephew, a truck driver, had arrived with the U-Haul carrying our furniture. He was impressed at our new home.

The kids lit up with excitement, they ran from room to room like little puppies.

After cleaning up, we went to eat at a buffet nearby. The buffets became a habit. We clipped the two for one coupons from the newspaper and we could all eat for eighteen dollars. Before I came to my senses, our overeating habits caused us to blow up like balloons.

It was early December, midway through the school term. The next year round school track started in February. This gave us almost three months to settle in and familiarize ourselves with the area.

Our day started with cleaning house, a light breakfast and jumping in the car with a map to go sightseeing for hours. Then we would head for the buffets before three to get the lunch prices.

Our first Christmas was excellent. Not many toys but

lots of fun.

I had Legal Guardianship of the three youngest children but not the two teenage boys. Therefore, I could not enroll them in school. Their father was supposed to take them but he never showed up.

My daughter Pamela and her husband Clarence took them and enrolled them in school in California. I will forever be grateful to them for their assistance in caring for Jeanine's sons.

Ellen and her twins were still residing in Fresno California. They came to visit us and fell in love with the place. The following year they packed up and moved to Vegas.

Jeanine was released from the hospital but was not doing well. She continued to abuse herself. She came for a visit and liked the place. She had very little money but had made up her mind to find an apartment during her visit. She asked us to take her to a Casino to play the slots. She invested twenty dollar and won enough money to pay first and last month's rent. A few months later, she had settled in an apartment near Ellen's.

It was good for the kids to be so close to their mother.

Retiring and Relocating

Go to now, ye that say, today or tomorrow
we will go into such a city, and continue there a year,
and buy and sell, and get gain:

James 4:13

Chapter 18
Jeanine Give's up on life.

After spending eight months in the hospital in California, Jeanine was happy to have settled in Nevada so she could be near her children.

Twenty-five years had passed since Jeanine fell victim to the wheel chair but she held on no matter what.

Now she was the mother of seven children, all born while she was in that wheel chair. I felt like I had given birth to all of them.

The two oldest were in college. Dana at Long Beach and Derrick at Chico State. The two boys Justin and Damion lived with Pamela and I cared for the three youngest children.

Jeanine had become accustomed to calling the ambulance for almost anything. The hospital staff was puzzled by her actions and did not know how to handle her.

She knew how to get her way. Besides being in a wheel chair, she had a diagnosis of anorexia and would gag whenever the nurse tried to feed her.

The doctors put her back on tube feeding to be force-fed.

Jeanine relied more and more on painkillers. She was five feet and ten inches tall and weighed less than ninety pounds. Because of the pressure on her buttocks, she was often bothered with decubitus ulcers. By the time we found out, she was in very poor shape and hospitalization was required.

She never gave up on looking good. Her hair was important and she always wore it shoulder length.

The young man that had been her boyfriend for a few years stood by her no matter what. He sold his car to assist her, Justin, and Damion in moving to Nevada. He gained employment at a car wash to support her and her two boys.

I had so much respect for him. However, the boys gave him a hard time and would not assist him in the housework. Yet he rode the bus to work and stopped off in the evening at a fast food place to bring food home for them.

The hospital informed us that they could not treat her anymore and she was sent to a convalescent facility.

Jeanine had been in some of those places and hated them. I remember her complaining about places she had stayed.

"Mother if I stay here another day I will act and look like them."

"Just look at her she used up a whole roll of toilet tissue wiping her butt."

"I am tired of looking at her behind. Get me out of here." "Why don't she know that she has not been to the bathroom?"

"I am just seventeen years old living with half dead people."

"I refuse to go to the dining room to eat. They make me want to throw up."

"Jeanine all of these patients have medical problems they cannot help themselves they are doing the best that they can. Do not make judgment. If they could do better they would."

"I hate it here. I want to go home."

"Jeanine you must complete therapy first, if you just cooperate with all of them it will make your stay shorter."

"Okay, I will try." She spent six months in that center and it left an awful impression on her.

Here we were twenty-five years later facing the same thing. I felt helpless at this point. She needed round the clock care.

I had her children to care for and was too old to give her the proper care.

The hospital informed me of the facility where they had sent her. It smelled so bad, the stench of urine lit up the halls. My heart fell because I knew that the first sight of me would send Jeanine into a frantic tail spend.

To my surprise, she just looked at me and said, "Hi Mother. This is my new home. Did you have trouble finding me?"

"No Jeanine. It is not too far from my house. Are you alright?"

"Yeah, I feel fine." She was nodding and slurring her words.

The nurse informed me that she had just received her meds and needed to sleep.

I returned the following day at dinnertime. When I saw what they gave her for dinner, I became so angry. I looked at all the patient's plates. Their meal consisted of a bag of potato chips, slice of white bread, a piece of baloney and a can of soda.

The head nurse told me that they do not feed the patient's heavy food after five o'clock because they give them a large lunch.

I knew that Jeanine would eat only the chips and soda. On the third day, Jeanine was sent back to the hospital where she stayed for several weeks.

I took the children to see her every day after school. The nurses liked the girls and would save food for them.

Her daughter Asia asked the nurse if she could spend the night with her mother. "I can sleep on the couch. Please?"

The nurse told her that she could if she promised to stay in that room and not wander in the halls.

She promised. "When my head hits the pillow I sleep like a baby and nobody can wake me up."

Her sister, ten-year-old Candice, wanted to stay also.

The nurse decided that they should take turns spending the night. Asia would spend Friday nights and Candice would go on Saturday nights.

I was perfectly happy with that arrangement. Jeanine needed to spend time with them. Her apartment was not too far from the hospital. Her sons Justin and Damion would walk across the field to visit their mother.

She completed her stay at the hospital and was sent to another facility. It was a long way for me to drive every day so I went every other day.

It was not as bad as the last place. There were other patients in wheel chairs. They would wheel themselves around the block, take smokes and laugh with each other.

Jeanie was not improving. She stayed medicated as much as she could. She ended up back in the hospital. This time it was a hospital on the other side of Las Vegas.

She informed me that she liked this place and had made good friends with her doctor. "Mother I want you to meet my doctor he is the best doctor that I have ever had."

"Good. Set up an appointment for me. I want to talk to

him anyway."

Before I could meet him, Jeanine came to a picnic at my house. She was allowed a home visit. It was the Fourth of July and my backyard was the focus of many of the nearby relatives to gather and enjoy the traditional barbeque with all the trimmings.

"Mother I want to talk to you." she grabbed my hand and squeezed it. "Can we go inside?"

I wheeled her chair to a bedroom and closed the door. When I looked at her, tears were running down her cheeks. I asked her what's wrong.

"Mother please don't be mad with me. I hate to do this to you but I am so tired. You have been so good to my children. But I can't take it anymore. I just don't want to go on. I am not going to get well. And I am asking you to not be mad with me."

"Jeanine, I don't want you to kill yourself. That is a sin."

"I have no intention of killing myself. All I need to do is let go and I will be gone it is that simple I just want your permission to let go."

"Jeanine. It is not left up to me. That is something between you and God. But I do understand your feelings. You have gone through so much. It takes a strong person to make it through what you have experienced. I don't think I would have made it this long. So what do you want me to do?"

"I do not want you to have a big funeral and I want to be cremated. And give the children my ashes. Don't spend much money. The kids will need it. I have already talked to my doctor about this. He knows that I will not get well. He wants to discuss it with you."

I met her doctor who gave me the rundown on her

condition. However, I had heard those same words before from many doctors.

Jeanine had lost more weight, down to sixty-eight pounds.

The doctor said, "Miss Pierson, your daughter has confided in me that she is tired of living like this. How do you feel about this?"

"Like I told her, it's in God's hands not mine."

"Are you familiar with hospice services?" he asked.

"Yes Jeanine has been in a hospice many times. She got out and had more babies."

He laughed and said, "Not this time. I know of a place that she can go." He gave me the address to go check it out.

I went home and called her son Derrick who was in college and told him that he needed to come home to see his mother.

Her daughter Dana had already arrived.

Derrick asked if he could come next week. "I am in the middle of finals and cannot leave now."

"According to the doctor she will not be here next week." I gave him my credit card number and asked him to come as soon as he could. "Make sure you tell your instructors of your emergency and ask them to give you another time to do your finals."

Jeanine called me and said that she had been transported during the night but she wanted to see Derrick.

"I've called him and his plane will be arriving tomorrow evening."

I informed the children of what was going on. And that they should all get dressed in their Sunday best and go to the hospice for a long visit with their mother.

Going through the motion of taking the children for a

final farewell took a toll on me. I fought back tears but had to keep a straight face.

Ellen arrived at the hospice and that took some of the pressure off me. That gave me the chance to slip to the bathroom and scream as loud as I wanted to.

Jeanine hugged and talked to each of the kids telling each of them to always listen to Nana and be good to her. "Make sure you give her the respect she deserves." She grimaced with pain and was given another injection.

That was the time for us to leave.

After arriving home, Derrick called for me to pick him up at the airport. We rushed to the hospice to see Jeanine. I knew that she was in her final hour from the look in her eyes.

Derrick entered the room.

She looked at him with a pitiful stare but she had lost her ability to speak.

Derrick gave her a big hug and said, "I am here now. I know that you are sick and tired. I just want you to know that it's alright to go on. We will be alright. We will all stick together. There is nothing more you can do. So go on to a peaceful place. It is time for you to get some rest."

Dana said, "I will stay here. I do not want her to die alone."

Derrick and I left.

As soon as I pulled the car into the garage, the phone rang. It was Dana calling to inform us that Jeanine was gone.

I will always believe that she waited for Derrick her first born to come before she made her exit.

Rest in peace Jeanine.

Jeanine Gives up on Life

Yea, though I walk through the valley of the shadow
of death, I will fear no evil: for thou art with me;
thy rod and thy staff they comfort me.

Psalms 23:4

Chapter 19
Sessy Battles Illness

Jeanine's passing changed my life and the children's attitude. Mama's voice echoed in my head. 'Sessy everything changes, nothing stays the same.'

The kids were growing up and I was getting older. It was hard to raise a big family now that I was in my seventies. I took it in stride and got involved in all of their school activities, knowing that they were adjusting to the loss of their mother. I tried to involve them in special activities to help them adjust and accept the fact that she would not be back.

The boys, Justin and Damion moved in with me because Jeanine's boyfriend moved back to California.

I had not allowed time enough for myself to mourn. I was so busy every day. The children were harder to control.

I took several classes in child development. My favorite was the one explaining the thirteen year old, which is the most difficult year. I learned that the hormonal changes in their bodies could send them into rages that they do not understand.

My days were long and hectic. I stayed irritated most of the time. The house was a wreck. I assigned chores for each kid but most of the time they were left undone.

Because of my age, I knew that this lifestyle could not continue. Something must change. Mama's words popped into my ears again. 'Where there is a will there is a way.'

Pamela and Clarence came for a visit and saw the chaotic situation I was enduring and offered to take all the kids and raise them.

"You mean you guys would do that? Take all of them? All six of them?"

"Mother you are too old to work so hard plus they are not listening to you anyway. I have never seen you look so tired."

"Are you sure Clarence won't mind taking on such a load? I would not want this to affect your marriage."

"We discussed it before we got here and we are together on this decision."

"I would be glad of the help and I know that my osteoarthritic knees would rejoice. Let them finish out this school term, which just started. That will give you time to be ready for the big change in your household and switch guardianship."

I knew that Pamela and Clarence were right and I was very pleased at their offer to help.

I made plans for a grand exit for the children--something that they would enjoy and never forget. This would be my way of saying goodbye to them and perhaps see them in the summer months.

While watching the television one day, I saw an ad offering a big discount package to Disney World in Florida. I investigated the offer and decided that it was over my head, far too expensive for my poor family.

While waiting in line at my car insurance company I saw another ad offering a package to Disney World. I picked it up and inquired for more information. I was told that they could assist me in utilizing the package by creating a monthly payment plan to make it feasible for me to handle. I signed the contract but did not tell the children of my plans because I wanted to be sure that I could handle everything in time for the trip.

I struggled with depression, but continued to get involved in all the children's school activities. All of their teachers knew me on a first name basis.

I searched the newspapers to find any free activities the kids could attend. Their favorite was the water slides, swimming pool and game room. I promised them that I would take them every other Saturday if they had completed their chores.

Everyone was excited except Asia. She had a room all by herself. I checked on her to see if she was up. She sat in the middle of the bed reading a book.

"Asia, you need to get up if you are going with us. We are leaving at 12:00 sharp."

She did not reply.

I left the room and checked on the swimming suits and towels.

Candice and Gina were making lunch for us to take to the water slides.

I waited for Asia to come down to pick out the swimsuit that she wanted to wear. She was taller and heavier than I am and she always had first choice. I went to her room to inspect as I had done for the others.

Asia had not moved and the room had not been touched. She was sitting in the exact spot that I had left her.

"Asia, what's wrong with you? This room is not clean. Are you going with us?"

She gave me the silent treatment and a mean look.

"I came to see what swim suit you want to wear."

She ignored me.

"Girl if you don't get up and clean this room you will be in deep trouble."

I looked around the room, picked up a wooden ruler, and tapped her on the shoulder. I was not aware that she was waiting to kick me. We always got along. I had less trouble from her than any of the others. I know the light peck on her shoulder was not meant to hurt her.

Asia Leaned back and kicked me directly in my stomach. I was stunned I could not believe she had kicked me.

She repeated the kick and started to curse at me. "You old bitch. I hate you! I wish you would hurry up and die with your old self."

Candice rushed into the room and said, "Stop Asia! Don't hit Nana."

I lost my mind. When I came back, I was told that I had snatched Asia off the bed by her braids and flipped her to the floor and stomped on her. I do not remember any of that. It must be what happened because she had bruises all over her.

"I don't want to stay here anymore. I am going to live with my sister."

Her sister had just completed basic training and was not qualified to keep her.

The police arrived and questioned all of the children. They searched the house. I don't know what they were looking for. Nothing out of the ordinary was found.

I paced the floor back and forth and refused to sit down. They called for the paramedic to check me out. My usually normal blood pressure had risen to 190 over 88. They wanted to take me to the hospital.

I said, "No. Take her out of here."

"Lady we can't do that. You are her guardian and she's your responsibility. When you tapped her with the ruler you opened the door for her to hit you."

"Oh, it's my fault now? You guy's will hit her with that Billy stick and crack her head if she kicks you but I am supposed to take it?"

The younger officer told her, "You had no right to hit your Grandmother. She is old and is still trying to take care of you. If we have to come out here again, we will take you to jail and you will not be able to come back here again. You should be ashamed of yourself. Look at this nice house you should want to keep it clean. Ma'am if she ever hits you again just lay her out with something bigger than a ruler. I will put that on record."

When Pamela got the news of what happened she rushed to get Asia and gave her a strong talk about how she cannot mistreat her grandmother. "That's my mother. I have never raised my hand to hit her and you do not have the right to abuse her like that. I will not allow you to stay in this house any longer you will go home with us."

Asia was removed the following day back to California.

My health continued to deteriorate I should have gone to the hospital to determine the damage to my intestine because I was still very sore.

The daily chores became almost unbearable. Picking up the big pots of food was painful. I had gained weight and was depressed.

I was still planning the trip to Disney World right after school was out for the summer.

195

One cold February night, chills, fever and sweaty clothes awakened me. The coughing was painful to my chest. When the morning came, I wrapped myself up and went to the Quick Care near my house.

I had Bronchitis and needed to rest for a few days and take the entire antibiotic. I felt better in a few weeks but relapsed repeatedly to a total of four times. I finally recovered and started back to my Tai Chi classes that I liked so much.

The time had come to talk to the children about the trip to Disney World.

"Hey you guys, what would you think about going to Disney World this summer.

They all said, "I want to go. I want to go."

"Okay. It will cost a lot of money. We can do if we all pull together. What I mean is all of you must do your part by not wasting the electric which means cutting the light off after using, doing all your homework on time, helping me with the housework and keeping the yard cut."

"Just doing what you are supposed to do anyway."

We started packing early for our trip, which was for seven days. Each of us had a checked bag and a carryon that totaled thirteen bags including the bag full of snacks from Costco. I cut little squares of black and white cloth and the children glued them on the luggage for easy identification.

I was running a little short for our meals. I asked each child to ask a close relative to give a donation toward the trip.

"Nana is taking us to Disney World in Florida. She is paying all the expense. We need to help with the meals. Please send me a donation. Thank you." Each child received enough money for their meals.

Asia apologized to me for the ill treatment she had inflicted on me and I had forgiven her. I sent for her to go on the trip with us. She was so much help to me she took care of the girls and I took care of the boys.

We arrived in Orlando mid-day and were shuttled to our Hotel, which was on the grounds of the park. It was perfect. So close to everything. We were all excited.

We changed, had a hot meal and spent the rest of the evening choosing our rides and eating-places for the whole week.

The children were so gracious. They helped me get on most the rides except the Ferris wheel and the roller coaster. That is not my thing.

"Come on Nana let's get on this ride."

"No baby. I will sit here and hold your belongings until you get back."

Antoine got hooked on the big turkey drumsticks. He bought one every day.

The Safari ride through the park was exciting until a big downpour soaked us to the bone. The entire trip was a blast we all enjoyed everything.

The following week Pamela and Clarence came to get the children but my freedom did not last long. I became ill with bladder problems that required surgery.

Ellen got herself together and came to stay with me while I made a speedy recovery.

I blamed myself for being ill because I had ignored my health to take care of others. I spent the next year practicing what I know. I walked, ate right, lost weight, took care of my hygienic needs and returned to Tai Chi classes and other classes to learn about new things.

School was out now and the kids were begging to come home. "You are at home. Please let us come home."

"No. You kids won't listen to me. You are better off with people that you respect."

Pamela and I decided they could come and visit me for the summer.

They were so polite and helpful in every way. They were working on being able to stay with me, the place they called home.

"Please Nana. Let us stay. We will be good. You will not have to do anything but cook. That's because we don't know how to cook. Please, please let us stay? You see how much we help you now? We will continue to help you. You have to rest more, let us help. We hate California. Don't make us go back."

One of them said, "If you make us go back I will run away."

Another one said, "Me too."

I prayed about the situation. I knew that I was too old but my heart went out to them. Plus, I was grateful to Pamela and Clarence for taking them to give me a break. At the time, I did not know that I would miss them so much. I had cared for them all of their lives.

Pamela called me and said to get the children ready because they were coming to get them.

"They do not want to go back and I decided to let them stay."

"Oh Mother, you are too old to keep them. Send them back. Just as we got them under control you want them back, that's not fair."

"Maybe not but I am afraid of being in this big house alone. Finding my expired body would not be cool."

They stayed with me and left one at a time. Everyone is over eighteen and doing well.

God has blessed me to reach the age of seventy-nine and still enjoy life.

Sessy Battle Illness

Preserve me, O God: for in thee do I put my trust.

Psalms 16:1

Chapter 20
80th Birthday Celebration

While walking to my brother's house nearly three miles away, I thought about my being seventy-nine years old. What can I do to top my last birthday? Oh, Yes. I know. I can throw a big party. I mean a big party. I had a very good friend coming from the Bay Area in California this weekend. I will ask her to help me to plan the whole thing.

Turning eighty years should mean something. Walking three miles uphill at age seventy-nine was fine but I wanted to top that. I called my brother and told him that I was walking to his house.

"Are you crazy? Let me come and get you now."

"Nope I can make it. Just be ready to make the apricot jelly when I get there."

When I got within two blocks of his house Dean was waiting for me to finish the climb.

"My God, girl! You scared me. It's too hot for you to walk that far."

"I did it. Now I am ready to make jelly."

Dean had planted apricot trees in his back yard that supplied lots of fruit. We made sixty-eight quarts of jams and jelly that day.

I had planned to walk back downhill to my house but changed my mind when Dean informed me that it was 105 degrees outside.

I thought about the party again. I should get started now. I called Pamela to run it by her she agreed that it was a great idea.

Creating a list of invites was a chore. I had made so many friends over the years how could I choose.

My birthday is in May--a pleasant time of the year in Las Vegas. I looked for places to celebrate and learned that none of them was what I wanted. So I decided to celebrate at my house.

My great artistic friend, Patty came for a visit from the Bay Area in California. She worked out a logical menu for the three-day party. Designed all the table set ups, designed the invitations and had them made, created a video of my life and gave me a sense of pride for sharing my home with my friends. She is such a good friend I just love all of her visits.

Pamela's friend, who is my play daughter, Rena from New Jersey, arrived a week early to assist me in getting ready for the party. She worked hard to get things done. We went shopping for the food and she was so good at what she did, getting things right, taking so much pressure off me.

The party took place over three days.

Thursday: Pick up arrivals from the airport and give directions to families traveling by car from out of state. Meet and greet party with a menu of spaghetti, barbeque, hot dogs and finger foods.

Friday: Prepare the food for the main event. Decorate the garden with clear lights placed in the trees and shrubbery. Put up torches around the fence and decorate each table.

This night was family night. All of my children, grandchildren, brothers, nieces and nephews and many cousins made their way to my home. It was the epitome of joy watching the families get together, seeing that they had truly missed each other.

We had the food and drinks catered in, leaving lots of time for board games, charades, card games and electronic games. We are so competitive with each other. The war was on that night.

"I hate to brag but I am the scrabble champ," I said. No one would play me by the end of the night, even though I promised to let them win.

Late into the evening, everyone was exhausted. Only the little ones went to bed. Everyone else grabbed a pillow and slept wherever they could find a place to lay their head.

Saturday: The big day have arrived. My 80th Birthday celebration. The party was set to start at six o'clock and end at ten. The assembly lines moved fast. Outside, the men grilled meats to perfection. Inside, the ladies cooked pans and pans of foods. The salads and fruits were prepared last.

My brother Dean baked nine large sweet potato pies. Many local friends brought desserts. They had asked me to let them help in some way. We had no time or space to prepare dessert, so their help was right on time. My granddaughter, Candice, set up SKYPE to share the event with friends unable to attend the celebration. My good friend Wilma surprised me with a large birthday cake. It was so tasty and beautiful.

Music and happiness lit up the house. My grandchildren were the hosts, greeting the guest, assisting in parking their cars and making sure that they were recognized as they entered the house.

By seven o'clock, at least 130 people had arrived from eight states and locally. I was one of the happiest people in the world.

The torches around the fence glowed to life as the sun descended in the west and the lighted trees and shrubbery came forth. I felt like I was in a magic forest surrounded by my friends.

The feast began. Rena had added seafood to the menu, Ling-su made Korean food, Hispanic and Italian appeared. Of course, I made down home soul food.

The minister from my church blessed the food.

"Oh I know there is a God." I was too excited to eat.

After dinner, Pamela made an announcement. "Will every one come in close? As many of you that can, bring your chair near the door or stand nearby." She motioned for everyone to gather round. "Mother, will you come and sit here?" she said, placing a chair in the center of everything.

"Girl, what's going on?"

"Oh, come on Mother. Just sit here."

I sat firmly in the designated chair.

Pamela took me by the hand and said, "Mother. You have spent most of your life helping others. You have been a role model, a friend, a caretaker and never asked anything in return. I did not know what to give you for your birthday. You do not need anything. You already have what you need or most of your friends have given it to you anyway."

Pamela reached into a pouch and pulled out a black leather bound 15x12 book. The front cover had a photo of me standing in a Tai Chi pose. Inside were pages and pages of letters from my children, grandchildren, my siblings, cousins, friends from my church and Tai Chi class, clients from the salon, and many people that I had met over the years.

As I sat there holding this thick book I fought back the tears. I must have done a lousy job because someone gave me a tissue.

Pamela explained that the book was too large to read in its entirety because many of the letters exceeded the length that she asked for. Therefore, she had asked four ladies seated near me to read excerpts from a few of the letters.

It began with my siblings.

> *Dear Sessy,*
> *Happy 80th birthday. Psalm 90:10....*
> *some family members said you and I were in*
> *competition to see which would become the better*
> *entrepreneur. We both excelled, you took the full*
> *service beauty salon route and I took the full*
> *service real estate route. We both trained workers*
> *and provided jobs for our communities. You are*
> *still working. I had to retire to cancer but I am*
> *okay now. Have a great birthday.*
> *Love you Sis! Your brother George.*

> *My sister Sessy.*
> *I am 7 years older than you, but we have*
> *always been close. No one can do my hair like*
> *you. Do you remember what you did to me when I*
> *was 16 and you, 9? I tried to chastise you and*
> *you were not going to take it one bit and you tore*

my clothes off. I stood there topless and the rest of my clothes were in shreds. I wished you had just slapped me and left my clothes alone. What made matters worse, Mama saw what happened. I was disappointed to see Mama laughing hysterically and do nothing. Happy 80th Birthday. Your sister, Maxine

Dear Sessy (I mean Shelly that's what I always called you.),

Happy 80th birthday. We always did things together when we were growing up. There were things I could not do and you would always do them for me or you would teach me how to do it myself. Sessy what I admire most about you is your courage. No matter what you had to go through you just kept right on going with your head held high.

Your sister, Crystal

To my sister Sessy,

As a child, you were the only one of my siblings that our father never spanked because you always behaved the way our parents wanted us to behave. Only God could make a heart so big for a person so small. I wish you good health and wealth always.

Your brother, Larry

Letter to my sister Sessy,

Sessy you have been both mother and sister

to me since I was 11 years old. When Mama died, you took me under your wings and sent me to school at your expense. You moved to California to make a better life for all of us. You sent me to collage and I became a photographer, all at your expense and you have never asked for anything in return. May God bless you to have many more birthdays.

Your brother, Dean

Happy Birthday Mother.
Blue skies, warm springs or summer winds, green grass bordering a vegetable garden. I was two years old when my vivid memory of my mother was formed. We were in the back yard you placed me on the ground beneath the clothesline. The skirt you wore gently danced across my head as you hung the clothes. You would frequently look down at me with a clothespin in your hand and pretend to affix it to my nose. I would laugh so hard it would make you laugh. I am now fifty-six years old and you have been the rock of stability in my life. I would like to congratulate you on a life well lived. I love you Mother. Happy 80th Birthday.

Your son, Tony. P.S. You are still a spring chicken in my eyes.

Happy Birthday Mother, Motha, Ma.
Thank you, Mother, for providing me with an amazing childhood. I have so many fun filled

*and exciting moments to remember. Every year
On December 26 the day after Christmas, we
would drive to the snow and rent snowmobiles,
sleighs and toboggans because it never snowed in
Berkeley. Our annual day was filled with so many
memories. As a child, we always played outside.
Our games were hopscotch, baseball in the middle
of the street, hide and seek, ride bicycles or
skateboards and we had our own tetherball in the
back yard. Rainy days meant staying indoors
playing indoor games. You knew how to make us
smile by the smell of Teacakes baking in the oven.*

*I thank you for being the amazing cook that
you are and for passing your recipes on to me.*

*You keep everyone laughing. The funniest thing
that I remember is on one of many trips to
"Funhouse" in San Francisco when Waldo tricked
you on one of the rides. You went up the long-long
flight of stairs to rescue Waldo because he was
afraid to come down. You sat down to rest and
Waldo said, "No mother. You cannot sit there."
You jumped up not knowing that he was putting you
in the right position to slide down. Waldo gave you
a big push and down the slide you went. You
screamed so loud everyone in the building turned to
see who was making so much noise. By the time you
made it to the bottom of the slide your dress was
over your head exposing your underwear. You
pushed your dress down, sat up and shook your
head with your glasses hanging across your face.
You got off the ride walking like you were in a
drunk stupor. Thanks for all the laughs.*

You have always been the essence of "Queendom" and it has been a privilege and honor to be your princess.

I will always love you. Pamela

Dear Mother,
When I first came to this country, I did not have any friends other than your son. I did not speak English and I missed my family deeply. Immediately you welcomed me into your home with opened arms. You have been like a second mother to me. I have learned so much from you and I appreciate your advice and long talks. Your friendship means so much to me and I am honored to call you Mom. You will always be part of my family no matter what the circumstance may be.
Love Ling-Su

Motha,
You are the light that kept me moving forward during the times I was ready to give up. I know that I am still on this earth purely by your prayers. When I think of all the things that you have been through, I know that no matter what I can't give up. I also thank you for all the fun filled hilarious trips we took every summer. Motha, you are the greatest. I have a lifetime of good memories because of you. Not only were you a number one mother to your own children you were a number one mother to so many others. I love you with all

my heart.
Your baby girl, Ellen

Mom
I have been witness to a person who truly embodies what it means to embrace family. To embrace both children and grandchildren in spite of their faults—selfishness, pettiness or just acting downright stupid. Wow, you are truly something Mom. You are both Saint and Queen. In spite of all the odds against you, you have loved with compassion and understanding that defies the obstacles placed before you. No, Mom. I don't believe in a lot of things...but I believe in you.
Love, Your Son-In-Law, Clarence

Dear Nana,
I am proud to have such a strong black and independent grandmother that is worthy of admiration. Growing up I witnessed how determined and self-sufficient you are and I aspired to live my life in a similar way. I admired how hard you fought to save our family and how you never gave up on any of us. We share the same love for education family and independence. You have always accepted me for who I am and that means more to me than I can express through words. I can only hope to have such a fulfilled and meaningful life as you are living now. Happy 80th Birthday and more to follow. You are the strength

*and backbone of this family and we would be lost
without you.*

Much love always. Your granddaughter, Mira

Dear Nana,

*I just wanted to say, you mean so much to me. I
appreciate all the things you have done for me. You
did not have to do it but you did. You are an
amazing person. I hope you have a great birthday.*

Love, your granddaughter, Candice

Dear Nana,

It's your 80th birthday. I hope you have the
best party you've ever had. Of all of my fifteen
years, you have been one of the nicest people that I
know. You let me stay in your home through good
times and bad times. You will always be like a
second mother and I appreciate that a lot. So I
want you to have the best time of your life during
your 80th birthday.

Your grandson, Antoine

Thank you, Nana.

*I want to thank you from the bottom, top and
side of my heart for all the things you have instilled
in me and the sacrifices that you made to take care
of all of us kids. Even in a house full of kids, you
still made time for me. All the little projects we did
together meant so much to me. You*

211

*gave us confidence and strength and we all know
where we got our good looks from, you. So the
things you have instilled in me have made me into
a strong and proud black man that I am today.*

Your Grandson, Cory.

Nana,

*I open the door, step out of the back seat of the
car and breathe in the cool fresh ocean air of
Berkeley California. It's a very familiar house.
The sight on this street and smell in the air brings
what seem like a lifetime of memories fluttering in
my young mind. I eagerly step onto the sidewalk
carrying my little bag filled with weekend clothes
and begin walking up the path that split the green
lawn and leads to the door of this house that
almost feels sacred. The same path that my dad
walked as a little boy. The same green lawn that
he played on in a black and white photograph.
Now it's me in that picture a generation later. I
step on the porch and peer back. Mom and my
sister are still getting stuff out of the car. Mom
shouts to me to hurry and knock on the door. I
know exactly what's going to happen as I have
taken this trip many times from Marina but each
time I am still flushed with excitement. I hear
footsteps approaching followed by the door
flinging open. Here it comes. My lungs are
warmed with the delicious aroma of collard
greens, sweet potatoes, fried chicken and
cornbread. My ears with the soulful voice of*

Nana greeting me. She hugs me with strength that feels powerful enough to crush my little frame but gentle enough to console a crying baby. I walk into the house to more familiar faces. Cousins, younger and older, aunties, friends, neighbors and enough food for a feast. I know it's going to be a good weekend.

These are a few of the great memories you have blessed me, and the whole family with over the years. Have a great 80th birthday
Your grandson, Cory.

By this time, I am whooping and sniffing, my nose and eyes both running. Tissue is coming at me from all directions. It is hard to express the joy and pleasure that I feel.

What a blast and so many letters. Thanks to all of you that took the time to express such warm feelings of love and appreciation for me. Some of you have been my friend for over fifty years. To enter all of your letters would have made this book too large. Therefore, I will make an effort to publish all of them in the near future. My book of memories will give me many hours of pleasure as I read each of them.

Thanks to all who brought or sent lovely gifts in my honor for my 80th Birthday. I will forever be grateful.

80th Birthday Celebration

I have been young, and now am old; yet have I not seen the righteous forsaken, nor his seed begging bread.

Psalms 37:25

Chapter 21
The Final Turning Point

February 2012, almost one year after my 80th birthday, my heart raced. I thought my flight was tomorrow, not today, so I was running late.

This trip wasn't at all what I had expected, but I stayed true to my commitment and stayed the entire month.

I was worried about not having a boarding pass and missing my flight. The hassle to get on the plane was quite unsettling for me. I felt that my 81 years had finally caught up with me.

I boarded the plane, plopping down in the first seat available, which was all the way in the back of the plane. I was leaving LaGuardia Airport in New York, and heading back home to Las Vegas, and God knows I was more than ready to leave.

It was cold, so I wore my heavy grey coat, boots, black wool scarf and a grey wool beret. I felt stuffed in my seat. I rested my head and let out a big sigh, "Wow, I made it!"

Questions ran through my mind needing answers. I wondered if I was becoming senile, or if my short-term memory loss was the beginning of Alzheimer's disease.

What have I done throughout my life that would make anyone give me such awful treatment? I fought back the tears and was glad the darkness gave me the chance to cry

215

unnoticed. I felt pity for myself and wondered, is this the end for me?

I didn't expect this and felt ashamed because I hadn't seen it coming. I needed a distraction from all things negative. I opened my laptop and played Scrabble, which was always my escape from reality.

My plane was 40 minutes late getting into Milwaukee and missing my connecting flight would mean a long layover. Please, God, hold the plane.

I rushed off the flight and an agent was waiting at the door. "Are you going to Las Vegas?"

"Yes," I said.

He grabbed my carryon bags and called the gate agent, "She's almost there--just give her a minute."

I was the last to board the plane before the door closed.

I didn't want to think about my life right now. I tried sleep, which didn't come. I had about four and a half more hours. I couldn't help but look back on my life.

I remembered my mother telling me, 'You reap what you sow'. I had also taught my children and grandchildren the same principles. I knew I hadn't always sown the right seeds but nothing I had done could have prepared me, or justified, the treatment I had just endured.

This was the turning point in my life--a true wake up call. There had been many turning points, but unfortunately, I made U-turns and allowed myself to be wrapped around the same warped poles that kept me from taking care of me.

One major turning point was when my mother, Sophia, died of cancer and left me in charge of keeping the family together. 'They'll listen to you. Make sure no one gets lost'. I was only 22 years old at the time.

I stayed near my mother's bedside comforting her and

clinging to her every word. I have lived my life ensuring that I did everything she told me to do, especially when it came to family. I used her words as my guiding light to travel a path that would help me to be a good person and teach my children to be good people. Or, so I thought.

Dana, my granddaughter, got a promotion with the U.S. Government. She moved from Texas to New York, where she purchased her first home. She would have to commute to another city and she hadn't yet obtained arrangements for her daughter's transportation to school and after school care. So she asked me to come to New York for a month.

I willingly accepted and Dana bought my plane ticket.

When I got to the airport in New York, my great-granddaughter, Lilly, was so glad to see me, as I was her. We grabbed one another, hugged, kissed and wiggled in each other's arms. She was screaming, "Nana, Nana!"

Dana hugged me and seemed genuinely happy to see me.

We began the long drive to Dana's house. She talked about her new home and how she liked the area, but didn't like the long drive to work. As we talked and drove, Dana got lost.

I said, "I'm starving! You know I've been traveling for twelve hours and all I ate was some mini pretzels and cranberry juice."

Dana didn't respond and I didn't make a big deal of it since I don't ever eat fast food.

It took us about an hour and a half to get to Dana's house. When we got there, I headed straight for the kitchen and opened the fridge to find it empty. Hunger hit me as if a ton of bricks had bypassed my brain and hit my stomach! I couldn't believe it.

I checked the freezer and although slight, there was food there, but it was frozen and it was ten o'clock at night.

Dana prepared some leftover noodles for Lilly and handed me the portion of her lunch that she hadn't eaten. I was still hungry when I finished. She gave me some of the noodles and a slice of lunchmeat and went to bed.

I was crushed and hungry. I sadly headed for bed.

I was so proud of Dana's accomplishments at such a young age. The house was beautiful, a two-story home with hardwood floors throughout. My bedroom was small and the ceiling came down at an angle, where the head of a twin bed nestled against it.

Underneath the bed were two drawers of Lilly's clothing. To the right of the bed was a small, clear three-tier bin. Lilly's closet was full of clothes given to her by friends and family members.

I was so tired I slept like a baby. Dana got up about five the next morning. Lilly got her lunch and we left to drop her off at school.

Dana drove her boyfriend's Ford F-150, a large 4x4 truck. She turned this corner and that as I tried to write down the directions for my next trip, alone. Some turns I missed because she was too quick.

After we dropped Lilly off, Dana stopped for muffins and we went back to her house so she could leave for work.

When Dana was ready to go, I said, "I don't want to drive the truck, it's too big. I don't feel comfortable about that. Why don't you let me drive the car?"

She left the keys for the truck and walked out the door for work.

I spent my day working on my book and checking out the house. I pulled some food from the freezer and cooked a meal. I was surprised when I went to pick up Lilly that I didn't get lost.

When Dana came home that evening, I told her that dinner was ready and we sat, ate, and had some conversation about our day.

The next morning, I again told Dana I didn't want to drive the truck but she left without the truck again. I dropped Lilly off for school, found a grocery store and bought a few things to cook.

Picking Lilly up from school that evening wasn't as simple as before, I got lost.

The next day, I woke up to snow covering the big truck in the driveway.

The phone rang and Dana said, "Oh! The snow scraper for the windshield is on the passenger side of the truck, on the floor."

What the hell am I going to look like, an 80-year-old woman with bad knees trying to scrape ice off a big truck? Now, I was stuck with this big, fat truck, snow, ice and hurt feelings...a recipe for disaster.

I opened the door, stood inside the vehicle with half my body hanging out and scraped the ice off the windshield. It took some doing, but I finally got to the other side and scraped the ice. Fortunately, I got Lilly to school safely.

Later that day, when I went to pick Lilly up, I couldn't find a parking space. I drove around the school twice, but still couldn't find a space, so I ventured over to the parking lot of the Muslim Church. A van had double-parked and I tried to squeeze past it. The side-view mirror hit the van. I tried to back up, but it didn't help. I got out of the truck and noticed a police officer behind me.

"Looks like you've had a little accident, huh?"

219

"Yes," I said. "I need to pick up my great granddaughter at the school across the way." I began to panic.

"Go ahead and get her."

"I can leave the truck here like this?" It sat haphazardly positioned against the van.

"I'm the police, whose going to complain?"

I said," all right." I ran off to get Lilly from school.

As we walked up to the van, she exclaimed, "You wrecked Arthur's car? I'm going to tell him!"

"You don't have to tell him. I'll tell him."

"No, I'm go to tell him," she said.

I now faced with the daunting task of calling Dana to tell her that I had wrecked the truck and needed the registration and insurance information. Although I had asked her for the information before, I couldn't find it. I kept pulling out old registration cards, but never found the insurance card.

The officer took the old registration form and transferred the information to the report.

I drove home and later confronted Dana about the truck. "I don't like driving that truck. Here's my credit card, just rent a car for me for the next three weeks and I'll drive it until I leave."

She said nothing. The next morning, she left the truck and she drove her car to work.

I was dumbfounded as to why she was treating me with such disdain. I had loved her and cared for her all her life. If she needed anything, I would try to make sure she got it. When she graduated from high school, I motivated her to go to college, bought her a computer, and gave her money for things for her dorm room.

Her parents weren't dead but I was very much the primary parent for her and all of her siblings. Again, I was here for her, over thousands of miles from the comfort of my home, and she was treating me like a servant with no right to understanding, compassion, or dignity. I felt hated by my own granddaughter.

Dana had scheduled me on a connecting flight from Las Vegas to Atlanta to New York--her eighty-one-year-old grandmother! What the hell was she thinking?

I came out here as a favor to her, not because there was something I needed from her. I paid for the gas for that big, monstrous truck, even though I was taxiing her daughter around. I didn't mind helping, or driving Lilly around. I love her, I love them both. I didn't mind cooking dinner, or making sure Lilly ate her food. But, I did feel used and taken advantage of. I didn't appreciate her telling me I couldn't use the bathroom downstairs because it was too close to the kitchen. At 81 years old, I was not going to walk up and down those hardwood steps to use the bathroom. Not with this bladder!

The visit wasn't all bad. Dana took Lilly and me out to dinner at a very good soul food restaurant. In fact, it was so good, I wanted to go again, so I paid and we ate there again. Lilly and I went for walks almost every day. We played games on my laptop. In fact, she taught me new things on the laptop. We also created a big snowman that lasted a week. I tried to be a good grandmother as I had been before.

I now realize everyone has turning points. It's my responsibility to recognize when to let go and let God look after them. My eyes had been opened to the fact that I needed to spend more time looking after myself. Like all mother's and grandmother's, I neglected my own needs putting everyone else first. It was finally time for me to care about me.

221

The Turning Point

Surely goodness and mercy shall follow me all the
days of my life: and I will dwell in the house of the
Lord forever.

Psalms 23:6

Chapter 22
Tony's Untimely Death

Hello Motha. Are you watching the campaign? What do you think? Tony I am getting scared. It looks too close. The Red states are popping up all over the place.. Yes they are. "I am at a friend's house right now. I'll call you back later. Love you, Mother." "Love you too, Tony."

I yanked on my Obama shirt and continued to pray. Oh, Lord. He has to win. Please Lord. Tension was high.

I began to talk to the television. An announcer on CNN said in a joyful voice, "Obama just won re- election."

"Oh! He won! He won!" My screams filtered throughout the house.

My granddaughter Candice ran down the stairs. "What's wrong with you?"

I grabbed her and gave her a big hug. "He won! Obama won!" I started what you might call my holy dance.

Candice turned around, left the room, and didn't return. "Hey, Nana? I want you to see this lady on You Tube." "Who is she?" I took one look and realized that is was me.

She had captured me, acting out of character like a wild woman, with my hair standing up all over my head. "Girl, if you don't take this picture off You Tube I will kill you."

"Nana, it's not on You Tube. I was just playing. I would

not do that to you."

"If you had just told me I would have combed hair silly girl."

I waited a week or so hoping Tony would call me. I had not heard from him in weeks. I called his number. It was not a working number.

More weeks passed and I began to get worried. When Christmas came and went with no card or phone call, I began my search to find him.

I called Tony's daughter Mira. She had not heard from him in a long time but was trying to locate him also.

I found the number of the only person in San Diego that I thought would know where to find him. Her name is Raynell. She expressed concern because she had not seen him in while either then assured me that she would find him.

They had been friends for nearly nine years. She knew most of his friends.

About the fifth day, she contacted me. "Miss Pierson I found your son. He is in the Hospital very ill in the critical care unit in San Diego. You should come as soon as you can."

I called Mira who lives 70 miles before San Diego and told her that Candice and I would be stopping by her house the following day, on our way to see her father Tony.

Ling-su, Tony's estranged wife, and his son Ray who lives in Northern California met us at Mira's house. We went to the hospital together.

The closer we got to the hospital the louder my heart thumped. I wanted to hurry in to see Tony. Yet I was afraid.

I talked to his doctor who filled me in on what happened. He said that Tony had been eating, and because of the problems with his pancreas, he vomited and passed out. He continued to vomit while he lay unconscious and some of it got in his lungs. Someone called an ambulance. He was taken to the hospital and he had been unconscious ever since. While in the hospital, he contracted pneumonia.

I said I was his mother and I planned to take him home with me after they released him from the hospital.

The doctor said, "I'm sorry but you will not be taking him anywhere. He is too sick to be moved."

Oh my God, my God, I will not give up on Tony.

He had called me so many times saying he wanted to come home.

I would always say, "Come home. We could help each other. Lord knows I could use some help."

"Oh my God. What is all that stuff on him?" His thin body lay motionless on the ventilator. At least thirty hookups were attached to his body.

I wanted to help him. What could I do? I covered his foot with the blanket, rubbed his face, and talked to him. "Tony. This is mother. I came to check on you. You know you must get better so that I can take you home with me. You have always told me that you wanted to come and be with family. So here I am, just waiting for you to get better."

He looked so lifeless. I left the room and burst into tears, composed myself and returned.

I had prayed and prayed to God. "Please save my son. I know he is in your hands and I put my trust in you." My heart was broken and I was at my wits end. I felt like I was losing my mind. I had just lost my brother Larry two months ago and my niece Mary four months before.

I continued to pray, "Please Lord, this is my last son...

225

my last son! I know only you can save him."

The only thing left to do was pray and walk the halls in the Critical Care Unit and hope that Tony would at least open his eyes, make some kind of move to let us know that he was fighting for his own life.

I called my close family members and my Pastor to inform them of Tony's condition.

After talking to his Doctor, I begin to feel like I had already lost Tony. He said, "If he lives he will be wheel chair bound and in a vegetative state."

Oh no. Tony kept himself clean cut, neatly dressed and he practiced good hygiene always. I knew that he would hate to live in such an incapacitated state. I was not prepared to see him go. Therefore, I put it in the hands of God. "God please let your will be done and help me to accept whatever is your will."

We took our daily trips to the hospital. Some days he showed improvement but other days it appeared that he was taking his last breath.

The doctor asked to speak to the family to explain our options for Tony's care. We could continue what they had been doing or stop the ventilator.

There was no way that I could make that choice, so I took myself out of the equation and left it up to his children Mira and Ray.

Of course, they could not make the choice to let him go.

Mira said, "I know my father wants to live. Just give him a little more time. Please give him more time." I felt so sorry for her. She needed to know that she had given her father every chance to live.

Ray, his son, was like me. We both felt like it was out

of our hands. We did not know what the right thing was. Ray did a lot of research to understand the prognosis and chance for recovery. The doctors were up front with him.

The family was called in again. This time I lost my mind. The Chaplain offered us help with prayer and sympathy. He asked each of to express our feelings and concern.

My feelings were that Tony was already gone and even if he had lived, it would have been a miserable life. I did not want to rush his exit or push for a prolonged painful existence. My other concern was what kind of burial to plan and what the cost would be if he expired tomorrow.

A few days later, we were told that he would not make it through the night. "If you want to say goodbye, do so before you leave."

"Tony, this is mother. I know that you are tired. You gave it a good fight, a real good fight. I cannot say goodbye to you, I just can't. I love you. I have prayed so hard for you to recover. You are my last son. I give you back to God so that you may find peace."

I held his lifeless hand and cried aloud for a long time. My heart was so broken. He was my fifth child that left before me. I always thought my children should bury me, and not I bury them.

All I could do now is pray. Just pray for all of us.

Candice could not stay away from her job any longer. She had taken two weeks off work to help me drive to San Diego. We left Tony in the same condition that we found him.

Being home felt wrong. I wanted to be near Tony. He may need me. I called the hospital twice a day.

Depression set in. Most of my days, I spent sleeping

227

and eating.

Tony was still on the ventilator. He was getting smaller and I was getting larger.

I wanted to be a hermit with just the Lord and me.

On the fifty-first day, I called the hospital. The nurses were always nice to me. This day she seemed a little withdrawn.

"This is Sessy and I am calling about my son Tony."

She said, "Hold on for a minute."

"Miss Pearson didn't anyone call you?"

I felt that I already knew what she was hesitant to tell me. I asked her in a slow quite tone. "Did Tony Pass away?" "Yes. He did."

"When?"

"About fifteen minutes ago. I am so sorry."

I do not remember hanging up the phone. I remember the flow of tears that seemed to be never ending.

In my mind, I could see Tony coming home from school smiling and sometime playing funny tricks on me. Watching him walk across the stage to get his diploma from high school. Seeing him the first time in his military uniform. Watching him get his first driver's license. Looking at his smiling face as he held his first grandchild. I could not grasp him not being alive. Not yet.

I called Pamela and gave her the bad news. I could hear the screams through the phone and knew that she was in pain because of the loss of her brother.

Ray, Mira and Ling-Su made all the plans for the funeral.

I was a basket case.

I could hear Mama saying 'Sessy take care of this family.' I've gotten older and now this family is taking care of me.

My two remaining children and a niece made sure to get me to the services so I wouldn't have to worry about driving myself.

My niece, Shirley, rented a large van in Oakland California. Pamela and Ellen split the expense and drove from Oakland to pick me and other relatives up to attend the services in Riverside.

The memorial was quite touching. I had given his children photos of Tony from the age of two to his last photo of him pulling his carry-on bag, coming off the plane to celebrate my 80th birthday.

His children made a slide show with the photos and played it at the service. Watching him being happy stopped some of the crying turning them into oos and aahs.

They gave Tony a military service in Riverside California.

After the services, we all congregated at Mira's house for a big dinner.

As I sat at the dinner table looking around at so many relatives that went out of their way to say goodbye to Tony, I thanked God for family.

"Almighty God, please, accept my son into your Kingdom."

Rest in peace Tony

Tony's Untimely Death

A time to be born, and a time to die; a time to plant, and a time to pluck up that which is planted

Ecclesiastes 3:2

Chapter 23

What I Learned On This Journey

This journey has led me down many roads. Some rough and rocky, some smooth sailing and others just downright unpredictable. One thing I can say for sure is that I always found a way out with the help of God. Being born into a family that leaned heavily on the Lord for help in times of need was common for the times. Therefore, I knew nothing else.

It is a pleasure for me to share some of the things that I learned on the way.

I am a proud mother, grandmother and great-grand-mother. Passing on some of my tried and true experiences it is my hope to enlighten you so you can bypass and avoid some of the pain I've suffered.

The first thing that I learned at an early age was the importance of family.

Looking back at the families in our communities as I was growing up, it became clear that the parents who spent time instilling good morals to their offspring created different results than the parents who let their children become villains.

I was involved in an incident that made my observation a reality. It was the last job that we could get before school started. It was called 'Cotton Scrapping', which meant picking the cotton that had been left or any new cotton that had opened.

Many of the families met at Tom's grocery store where a county school bus picked us up and took us to the fields to do the final cotton picking.

"Oh boy I can get my favorite twenty-five cent jar of peanut butter and ten cent box of crackers for lunch at Tom's store."

As I picked the bolls of cotton I thought of the good time I would have at lunch. We labeled and stored our lunch in the shack provided for our belongings.

One of our neighbors had lost control of her children, she would curse at them and they would curse back. Miss Augusta called to her son. "CJ get your ass over here and pick this cotton you little bastard."

C J shouted back, "I don't want to pick no cotton leave me alone you mother-fucker." He ran up and down the rows playing like a little kid--and he was thirteen.

She threatened to whip him but did nothing.

Whispers were heard from many of the parents, "I need him at my house just one day. I would kill him."

"No she is the one that needs killing. Look at what she is teaching him."

My mind was now counting down the minutes to lunchtime. Someone had to call out 'Yoo-Hoo lunch time' before we could stop.

I heard my name.

"Hey Sessy, look." CJ raised up an empty peanut butter jar shaking it from side to side. "It sure was good."

I dropped my sack and ran so fast toward CJ my run become afloat.

His mother was calling out to me. "Leave him alone. I

will get him. Leave him alone."

I sped faster like a wild antelope. When I reached CJ, I grabbed the empty jar and beat his head and face as long as I could see him.

He snatched away and took off running.

The applause from other workers brought me back to my senses. Yes, I had lunch. My coworkers shared some of their lunch with me. It was not like my peanut butter but at least I wasn't hungry.

CJ's parents never took the time to instill good morals in their children because they had not learned good morals themselves. C J was teased because he was a teenager that had been beaten by a nine-year-old girl. All of their children became terrible individuals.

This Journey of eight and a half decades has taught me that my faith in God is the backbone of my life. I have experienced miracles. So many have materialize right in front of me, no one else can validate his goodness. Would you call this a miracle?

One day I was driving home from class at San Francisco State College to my home in Berkeley. I knew I would be stuck in traffic if I did not make it to the Bay Bridge before three o'clock. Just as I was about to reach the freeway leading to the bridge my car slowed down right before the entrance.

"Oh no! I have to get on the bridge. Please Lord, let me on." I pumped the gas moved the steering wheel. "I can't stop here." So I pulled to the right in front of a service station.

Just as I was about to open the door and go inside the station to get help, I heard a big crash. Boom! A car was coming off the Freeway the wrong way. Had I entered, as I was rushing to do, we would have had a head on collision. Instead, the drunken driver hit a column under the bridge.

I prayed for the driver to recover. Then I went into the service station to get help to start my car.

The attendant asked me to get in the car and try to start it.

I turned the key and the car started right up. "Thank you, Lord for saving my life again."

God will take care of you if you do your best to care for yourself. It's our responsibility to take care of our health, mind and soul. Many of my friends have asked me, "How do you do so many things and in your mid- eighties?"

My day starts between six and seven in the morning. I fall on my knees and thank God for a new day. I take my dog, Louie, outside and stretch myself (Louie taught me that).I practice Tai Chi some days. When I return inside, I wash my face brush my teeth and do a little exercise. I brew a cup of coffee and while coffee is brewing, I eat a piece of fruit, turn the television on and get the local news. I walk out front and pick up the newspaper to learn of activities near me then go online to check my e-mails. I drink a cup coffee while I work the four puzzles in the newspaper: crossword, hocus focus, jumble and Sudoku. Then I eat an enjoyable breakfast and check my calendar to see if I have any appointments for the day and govern myself accordingly. If I feel like cleaning, I will. If not, I don't. I fill my day doing whatever I like to do. Whether it's working in the garden, reading a book or just whatever I want to do for that day.

I have learned to shake off the excess baggage that I carried around in my heart about the loss of five of my seven children that passed away before me.

I always wondered what I could have done differently in the way I brought them up. I gave it my all every way that I could. Writing this book helped me to understand that it was not my destiny but theirs. They lived out their designated time and there was nothing that I could do to change any of that.

I believe in the cliché of 'it takes a village'. I had a village. A village of church, school, and neighbors who's help was beyond valuable.

I would sit in church with my grandchildren and take up an entire pew. A few times the usher tapped me on the shoulder and handed me a check from one of the other parishioners. I later found out that they had a feeling that I could use their tithes more than the church at that time. I would leave my car open during services and people would leave gently used clothes for the kids. I never did find out who some of them were but I always thanked God for these anonymous angels.

In 2004, Unity Baptist Church decided to award a Mother of the Year award to someone in their congregation. I was one of five nominees. The congregation voted and I won. I felt so good and it gave me some validation for all my hard work.

All the teachers at the schools knew me because I stayed involved with the children's education. One Christmas, a teacher asked if I would be home the next day because Santa Claus wanted to come by the house and leave gifts for the kids. There were so many toys and clothes my whole living room was full. They even brought a bike or scooter for each child. We were so grateful and blessed.

This is a new day. Where is the Village? Did the new age of electronics steal it from us? Have we lost our face to face communication techniques? We have forgotten how to talk to each other. I do believe when someone comes up with an answer to this problem they will be awarded the Nobel Peace Prize.

I have learned from my mistakes, we all make them. Be forgiving and ask for forgiveness. Know that God will always answer prayer. The answer may not come when you want it or how you want it but he answers.

I try to learn about the world around me out of necessity because many of my friends my age have passed away. It is a good feeling to have so many young people calling me Mother, Nana or Aunt Sessy. I learn from them. They taught me to text, SKYPE, listen to many kinds of music and use electronic that I never knew existed.

I also learned that you cannot defy gravity. When I look in the mirror and see new wrinkles, I know that's part of my life cycle. Being in my mid-eighties, heading toward my nineties, I am grateful for what's left.

I accept the stares from friends that I haven't seen for a while. "Sessy! What on earth has happened to you? I have never seen you look so old."

I just laugh and say, "That's because I've never been this old."

I admire the liars who say, "Oh my God, Sessy. You haven't changed a bit." While I stand there with a jelly belly, drooping breasts and heavy eyes, wearing a long sleeve shirt to hide the flagging under arms and trying to locate the nearest restroom before I take my seat. I am still proud of myself and I look forward to celebrating my centurion year and the new things I still have to learn.

I don't sweat the fact that invitations stop coming in the mail because most of my friends have passed away and the ones that haven't can't remember their own names.

Each day is a blessing. I look for the joy and laughter that I can experience with the understanding that God has blessed me with longevity.

My new job is to be mindful of how I treat me, being careful not to neglect the body that God has given me. There is no one, I mean, no one, who can handle that better than I.

Life is beautiful at any age so embrace it every day. I am grateful to have lived a life to remember and look forward to living and learning many new things.

My name is Sessy and I am glad to be here.

What I Learned on this Journey

Trust in the Lord with all thine heart; and lean not unto thine own understanding. In all thy ways acknowledge him, and he shall direct thy paths.

Proverbs 3:5-6

About the Author

S hirley Sanders was born in Mississippi during the Great Depression. She spent over sixty years raising three generations of her family. Her father was African American and her mother was African American with Native American heritage from the Choctaw Tribe.

Shirley became a successful owner of three Beauty Salons. Her degrees were in Nutrition, Child Development, Consumer Education, and a Community College Lifetime Teaching Credential in Cosmetology and Barbering. She has also written health articles for a local magazine in Oakland, Calfornia.

CPSIA information can be obtained at www.ICGtesting.com
Printed in the USA
LVOW12s0137060814

397557LV00001B/1/P